An Illustrated Catalog
of American Fruits & Nuts

The US Department of Agriculture
Pomological Watercolor Collection

U

**UNION
SQUARE
& CO.**

NEW YORK

atelier éditions

Pathologist Merton B. Waite testing the validity of pear blight germs by inoculation on the Department grounds, July 1893.

Lost apples, electrical grapes, and pink blueberries

An introduction to the USDA's pomological watercolor paintings

BY Adam Leith Gollner

In 1910, the US Department of Agriculture (USDA) Bureau of Plant Industry released a special 136-page bulletin called *Experiments in Blueberry Culture*. The blueberry had not yet been domesticated. Though still feral, little understood, and "strangely overlooked," the blueberry nevertheless seemed to have commercial potential. For even in its native habitat, the swampy barrens of North America, the blueberry was already sweet and hardy—exactly the kind of edible plant the USDA's Division of Pomology was scouting for.

Pomology is the scientific study of fruit—everything from growing and propagation to botanical classification and disease prevention. As America's chief pomologist Henry E. Van Deman wrote in 1886, the year of the Division's founding, its aim was "gathering specimens of fruits and making drawings and accurate descriptions of the same for future use by the Department." Public outreach took the form of publications such as *Experiments in Blueberry Culture* and yearbooks that contained images intended to help taxonomists identify different fruit and nut varieties and ailments or pests that might affect them.

Over 7,500 watercolor paintings, lithographs, and line drawings were commissioned by the Division of Pomology between 1886 and 1942. This book collects a selection of the most beautiful. Aesthetically delectable as these images are, their primary purpose, in a time before the wide application of color photography, was scientific and documentary. The text of this volume also gives context on how and why the USDA Pomological Watercolor Collection came into being, as well as the role these images continue to play in the development of blueberries and other comestibles today.

In the 19th century, healthy orchards and fruit groves were viewed as crucial to national prosperity. The majority of Americans lived in rural areas, and small-scale fruit cultivation was commonplace. Most fruit plants, whether raised from seed, cross-pollinated, or grafted, have the capacity to hybridize. By the mid-19th century, the average US citizen needn't have looked farther than their own or their neighbor's backyard to find examples. As a result, the possibility of discovering or making more novel fruits grew into a widespread preoccupation. From 1820 until 1870 in New England, a frenzy for growing pears (or "an extraordinary degree of enthusiasm for pears," as the *Oxford Companion to Food* puts it) became known as "pear mania."

"Nothing in the circle of culture," explained *The Fruits and Fruit Trees of America* (1845), a bestseller that went through numerous printings, "can give

5

more lively and unmixed pleasure, than thus to produce and to create—for it is a sort of creation—an entirely new sort." In support of these fructifying efforts, the USDA's Division of Pomology was established "to oversee the collection and distribution of new varieties of fruits, and to disseminate information to fruit growers and breeders."

Experiments in Blueberry Culture was sent to farmers across the country as part of that undertaking. It had a life-changing effect on at least one—a 39-year-old cranberry grower in New Jersey's Pine Barrens named Elizabeth Coleman White. After reading the bulletin, White wrote to its author, Dr Frederick Vernon Coville, chief botanist of the USDA, explaining that she wanted to collaborate in efforts to harness the berry's agricultural potential. She had prime blueberry-growing land to offer, among other resources. And she felt certain that "swamp huckleberries" (as blueberries were called around her home in Whitesbog, New Jersey), if bred properly, could one day "yield large revenues from thousands of acres that today are wasteland."

Together, Coville and White set out to systematically select and cultivate promising wildlings. The best of the plants they collected and hybridized were, within the decade, available to consumers. In the wake of these successful trials, White became known as "The Blueberry Queen." One of the varieties she and Coville bred, the Stanley blueberry, is still ranked among the sweetest-tasting blueberries ever created; it remains available for purchase at nurseries to this day (see page 205). Every Stanley plant contains the DNA of bushes that wild-blueberry hunters in the Pine Barrens provided to White, as do other blueberry varieties currently being sold commercially. Today's global blueberry market is valued at $4.5 billion.

In their early experiments, White and Coville found not only sweet blueberries, they also found berries with unexpected qualities. "The outstanding characteristic of these hybrids was the variation in the color of their fruit," wrote Coville. As these crosses were themselves interbred, "the resulting second-generation hybrids showed a still more remarkable diversity of color." Capturing this spectrum of colors for posterity is precisely the sort of the reason the USDA set up its watercolor program.

Only 15 percent of White and Coville's hybrids expressed the color they sought most: light, sky-blue skin with a dainty bloom. Most were dark blue or deep purplish. A number yielded fully black fruit. They also stumbled on other bizarrely pigmented oddities: some with "a metallic luster like that of new aluminum ware," while others they classified as "albinos," with red cheeks, white backsides, and mahogany hues. These latter "horticultural curiosities," as Coville characterized them, both tasted good and looked appealing, if somewhat freaky. He thought home gardeners might want to grow them as novelties, but he doubted "any albino blueberry will ever acquire importance as a market fruit." Even so, Coville felt that two albino varieties, in particular, deserved to be named and studied further: the Redskin and the Catawba. Watercolor paintings were duly made of both, for documentary purposes, as was done with other promising cultivars. (A cultivar is a *cultiv*ated *vari*ety of a fruit, such as a Granny Smith apple.)

After Coville's death in 1937, geneticists at the USDA's blueberry breeding program remained aware of the Redskin and the Catawba, if only by name. Though both possessed unique and desirable qualities, they didn't catch on. In time, both went extinct. They were lost to cultivation—but they weren't forgotten entirely.

When pink-skinned blueberries started showing up as segregants in USDA research plots during breeding trials in the 1990s, scientists found themselves wondering what, exactly, Coville's albinos had looked like. "I knew that Coville had named those two albino varieties," says breeder Mark Ehlenfeldt of the USDA's Agricultural Research Service at Chatsworth, New Jersey, "but I had never seen pictures of them. I had no idea what shade of pink or red they were."

Around 2005, as Ehlenfeldt was completing trials on a pink-skinned blueberry that had, he'd noticed, "consistently attracted the attention of visiting researchers, nurserymen, and consumers," he finally managed to find out what the Redskin and the Catawba looked like when a fellow berry researcher mailed him a box that contained copies of the two paintings from the USDA's watercolor collection. "It was so fascinating to see them," Ehlenfeldt recalls. "The plants don't exist anymore, but the paintings grant you a vision of what they actually looked like." Though markedly different from his pink blueberries, it was useful for Ehlenfeldt to see exactly what it was that Coville had been talking about in terms of his albino and red-fleshed hybrids—partially because Ehlenfeldt's selections were themselves much more radical, especially a lurid Barbie-pink variety he released to the public in 2005, called the Pink Lemonade blueberry.

Though the Pink Lemonade blueberry is still generally under the radar today, it has proven immensely successful with nurseries, which have sold over a million plants since the cultivar first became available. With its distinctive appearance and a taste profile that is more floral and delicate than that of more usual varieties, Pink Lemonade blueberries will surely show up more in produce aisles over the next few years—a fitting next stage in the progress of blueberry cultivation that began over a century ago with the pioneering work of Elizabeth White and Frederick Coville.

The paintings of the Redskin and the Catawba (see page 206) were both done by James Marion Shull, who contributed over 750 watercolors to the USDA's collection. He was one of the most important artists in the program, alongside Deborah Griscom Passmore, Mary Daisy Arnold, Amanda Newton, Royal Charles Steadman, Ellen Isham Schutt, Bertha Heiges, William Henry Prestele, and Elise E. Lower. The work of all these artists is stored in the Special Collections of the National Agricultural Library, a 14-story brutalist building in Beltsville, Maryland, on the grounds of the Beltsville Agricultural Research Center. Many of the fruits depicted in the paintings are themselves preserved in America's National Plant Germplasm System (NPGS), which operates genebanks and germplasm[1] repositories across the country.

Looking at the artworks in this book is the visual equivalent of tasting the incredible diversity of fruit grown at these clonal germplasm repositories. It's important to remember that the images and the actual plants are both part of the same immense undertaking the USDA began in the 19th century: a concerted effort to understand and catalog the natural world, and fruit in particular. Notions of resilience and tenacity have always been central to the collection's mission. The paintings document what the fruits looked like, and the fruit itself—over 500,000 different plant types—are backed up by America's NPGS. These seed vaults are the country's primary agricultural insurance.

Over half the images in the USDA's holdings, fully 3,807 in total, are of apples—and the country's genetic apple holdings are found in Geneva, New York, a five-hour drive from my home in Montreal, Canada. Around 15 years ago, while working on my first book, *The Fruit Hunters: A Story of Nature, Adventure, Commerce and Obsession* (Scribner, 2008), I made my way down to the Geneva Apple Collection, which contains over 2,500 different types of apples.

On that autumn day, apples were in full season, and I was able to walk through the rows of apple trees, each different from the next, sampling to my heart's content. Some of them were as sweet as candied apples, while others were bitter and crabby. One variety tasted like raspberry pie, another like it had been infused with rose water, and still others gave off the distinct savor of fennel seeds or mint.

When I spoke that afternoon with the collection's curator, Phil Forsline (now retired), he explained that despite being surrounded by such a dizzying array of apples, his favorite one of all is the Honeycrisp, a variety that was only released commercially in the 1990s and has become massively popular since then. Large to the point of bulging, almost muscular, its flesh raring to burst from its fairy-tale-red exterior, it boasts an impeccably calibrated cell-level juice-to-crunch ratio. It's such a powerful example of modern genetic selection that it seems to shame every other apple in existence. It's a Hollywood A-list apple: sculpted, toned, hyperproduced.

There is no watercolor painting of the Honeycrisp in the USDA's archive; nor is there any need for one, as this apple is extremely available and technically documented down to every last nucleotide. But just as the collection illustrates changes in American tastes and aspirations, which often seem to be finding their way forward by looking backward, there are watercolors of a number of the best heirloom apples I tasted in Geneva that day: the Esopus Spitzenberg (see page 40), with a tangy-tart taste matching the delightful mouthfeel of its name; the Arkansas Black (see pages 50 and 51), the exact depth of its blackness verifiable in a quick glance at Deborah Griscom Passmore's impassioned depiction of it; or Cox's Orange Pippin (see page 38), a spice-flavored apple largely forgotten today but a century ago considered such a fine sweetmeat that British fruit connoisseur Edward Bunyard wrote, "This fruit needs no introduction or elegy," in his legendary *The Anatomy of Dessert* (1929). Bunyard considered Cox's Orange Pippin to be "the Château d'Yquem of apples." It's still available in the UK, but rarely seen in North America. And given how good a Cox's Orange Pippin can be, especially after it has aged a bit off the tree, merely gazing at the USDA paintings of it can set one's neurological reward centers aflutter.

The place of origin of sweet wild apples is the Tian Shan mountain range near Kazakhstan. Many of the apples in the Geneva repository were actually gathered there, in the wooded outskirts of Almaty and its surrounding areas. As Forsline explained to me, important genetic material in such fragile ecosystems is in danger of being lost every day, whether through deforestation or urban sprawl, or because of political instabilities. Plant repositories such as that at Geneva, which are part of a worldwide network of genebanks called the Germplasm Resource Information Network (GRIN), play an immense role in the conservation of global biodiversity. Without the efforts undertaken by Forsline and his colleagues and successors, much familial apple DNA might have been lost to science.

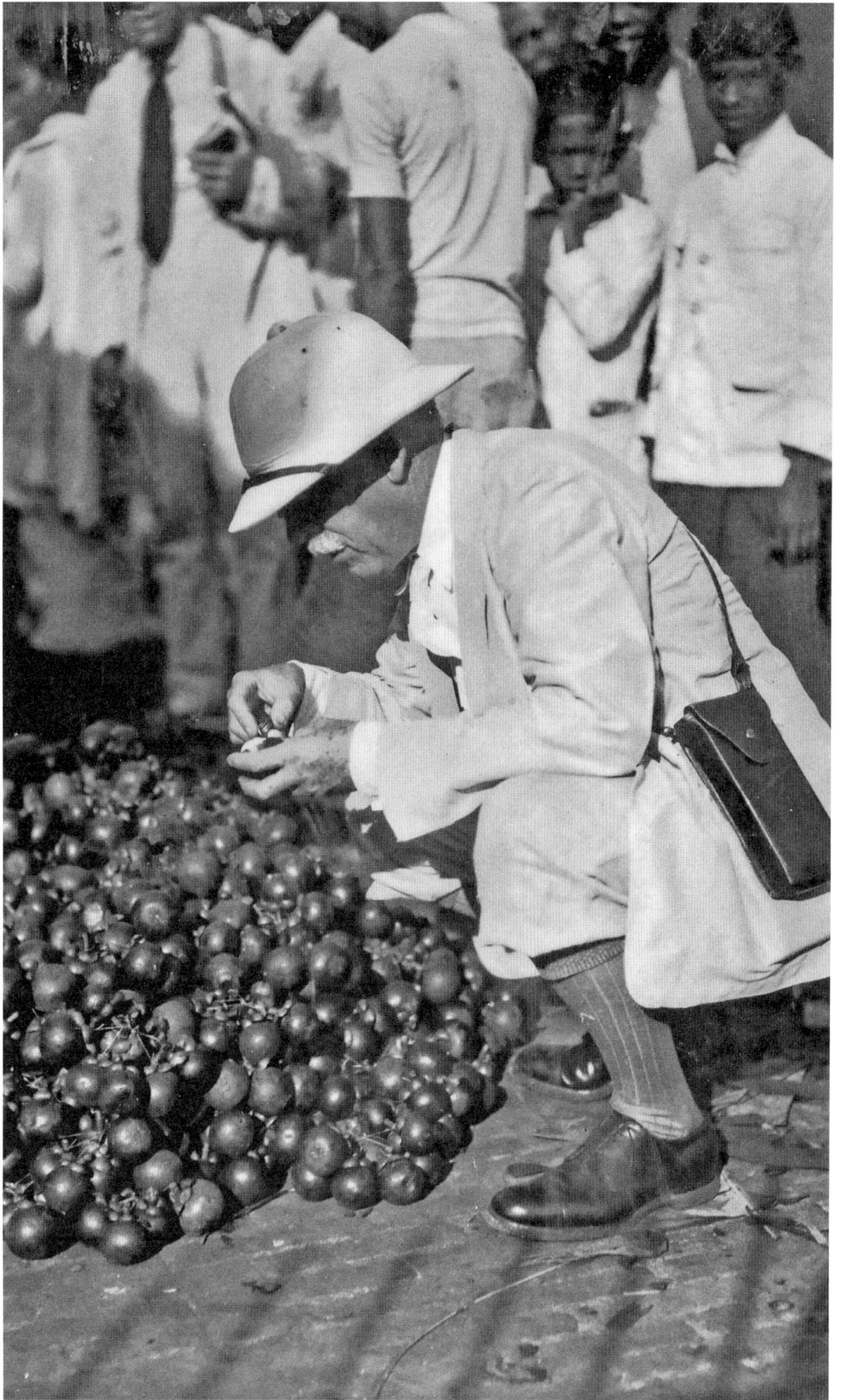

Dr David Fairchild examining and trying a mangosteen in a market, Medan Sumatra, A. V. Armour Expedition, c. 1926.

On the day of my visit to Geneva, I learned another fascinating detail. The greatest diversity in any given fruit species is always found in the place where it originated. For apples, it's Tian Shan. If a phytogeographer[2] were to search for an abundance of, say, wild pomegranates, their area of interest would be Iran. For wild melons, they'd know to go to Africa. Were wild bananas their quarry, Malaysia would be their first destination.[3]

Some years after the publication of *The Fruit Hunters*, I had a chance to visit both Georgia and Armenia, which happen to be the center of origin of grapes. Recalling the experience I'd had with apples in Geneva, I made my way to Saguramo village in Mtskheta municipality to visit Georgia's National Center for Grapevine and Fruit Planting Material. The facility, at the foothills of the Caucasus mountains, grows 425 varieties of indigenous grapes. Many of those grapes were at the peak of ripeness on the day I arrived, and I was allowed to stroll through the collection, sampling until my tongue turned purple.

There were yellow long-shoulder grapes (Mkhargrdzeli), pinkish-gray big eyes grapes (Mskhviltvala), and delicate bird egg grapes (Chitiskvertska). Some had turquoise skins stained with constellations of golden scars; others were perfect lavender orblets covered in diaphanous bloom. Clusters the color of burlap dangled languidly next to crimson bunches that seemed to glow from within. The fruits' sizes ranged from the tininess of blackcurrants to the heft of green Cerignola olives.

Trying them was a dreamlike experience—as is looking at the paintings of grapes in the USDA's collection (especially those made by William Henry Prestele, who completed a number of paintings originally intended to illustrate a monograph[4]). It seems to me that our imaginations, in contemplating these paintings (see pages 238–255), can tap into the sensation of what it is like to actually taste living versions of the images.

In Saguramo, I ate my way through grapes that tasted like ginger, tuna salad, celery, and cumin. One variety reminded me of something I can only describe as saffron-dusted leeks vinaigrette. Another was so bitterly tart it seemed to explain where the grapefruit got its name. They could be as starchy as potatoes or as turgid as little water balloons. Some were bland and leathery, while others had zingy, peppery interiors with cool seeds that seemed charged with an electric current. The Tsonori tasted like kumquat nectar. The Foxtail had the flavor of warm, flat lemonade. One unnamed wildling left a powdery taste on my tongue, like the sugary dust from the exterior of a marshmallow. I wondered whether any of the wild blueberries that White and Coville had selected for their breeding program exhibited that kind of icing-sugar residue. Either way, I felt the same way I do when flipping through the pages of this book: as though I had ended up in a kind of Hieronymus Bosch paradise of grapes.

Fruit-hunting and the procuring of plant materials from overseas has always been an integral part of the USDA's pomological mission. These specimens have to be gathered in their native habitats, often in distant lands. As USDA documents explain: "At the end of the 19th century, demand was high in the US for new crops that could diversify agriculture, replace imports, and grow in a variety of climatic and edaphic (soil) conditions. When James Williams became the Secretary of Agriculture in 1897, his first act was to send Niels E. Hansen of the South Dakota College of Agriculture to Russia, China, and other countries to collect alfalfa and other forage crops over a period of 10 months."

The USDA's Section of Seed and Plant Introduction was established the following year, in 1898. Working alongside the Division of Pomology, its motives were to "collect, purchase, test, propagate, and distribute rare and valuable seeds, bulbs, trees, shrubs, vines, cuttings and plants from foreign countries for experiments with reference to their introduction into this country."

The head of the Office of Foreign Seed and Plant Introduction was David Fairchild, a plant hunter who scoured the globe in search of valuable edibles. Fairchild's wanderlust also led him to write several books recounting his peregrinations; or, as he called them, "accounts of all kinds of romantic plant happenings." His finest book, *The World Was My Garden: Travels of a Plant Explorer*, received a 1938 National Book Award. In my own book, *The Fruit Hunters*, I summarized his collecting expeditions as follows:

> Whether having to drink water contaminated with dysentery or getting lost in impenetrable fever-infested forests, his misadventures were legion. Fairchild's junk caught fire in the South Seas. He "frequented most of the filthy places to be found in the world." When shipwrecked in Celebes, he came across one of fruitdom's great rarities: a hardened coco-pearl formed inside a coconut the way pearls form inside oysters. He ate dates in the Souks of Fez and the oases of Algiers. The last descendant of the Kings of Kandy taught him how to eat watermelon-sized honey jacks (far superior to regular jackfruit). In 1905, he married Alexander Graham Bell's daughter Marian. Together they traveled, finding yellow raspberries in Padang and the square, angular fruits of the *Barringtonia speciosa* in Mozambique. In Siaoe, dozens of softly singing children followed the newlyweds around the entire island.

In his position as head of the office of plant exploration, Fairchild was also responsible for finding others who could be dispatched to remote destinations—or, as he put it, "could tolerate all sorts of physical discomforts and walk thousands of miles where no roads existed." At first, these employees were called "Special Agents," but given the fact that they then tended to be treated as suspicious "food spies" abroad, the title was changed to "Agricultural Explorers."

Fairchild's envoy to Asia was Frank N. Meyer, a keen botanist and even keener walker, best and most obviously remembered today for discovering Meyer lemons (see page 110), which he came across in China in 1908. Meyer worked grueling hours, and often struggled to retain the guides and translators he hired to work with him. Over the course of his ramblings, he shipped tons and tons of plant materials back to the US. Musing on his efforts as a fruit explorer he wrote, "Life is so very strange and none of us really knows for what we have to go all through it." The only thing stranger than his life was his death: on a June evening in 1918, he disappeared from the deck of a boat crossing the Yangtze River to Shanghai. His body was found in the water by the city of Wuhu four days later. Had he killed himself? Had someone thrown him overboard? The mystery has never been solved.

To fill the post in South and Central America, Fairchild tapped an explorer named Wilson Popenoe. The biggest task Popenoe faced was to secure avocados in Cuba and Guatemala. As Fairchild himself would write, "Wilson Popenoe's explorations of Central America after avocados deserve to go down into history as one of the most thorough pieces of horticultural plant hunting work ever carried out, for he not merely secured seeds, which is a

Plant explorer Frank N. Meyer poses for a portrait during an expedition in China, c. 1909.

comparatively easy thing to do, but successfully landed here thousands of scions in such a condition that their buds could be budded into stocks waiting for them in Florida and California. This was long before the days of airmail."

Photos of Popenoe at the time show a handsome, slender young man wearing jodhpurs and a fedora. Even on horseback he wore a high collar, tie, and elegant suit jacket. In unpublished autobiographical notes, he wrote that he, "began to feel that plant hunting was just about the most romantic occupation imaginable. Not only did a chap get to travel in out-of-the-way corners of the world, but he stood a good chance of bringing home some new fruit, or food plant, which would add materially to his country's wealth and happiness."

But it wasn't all fun times. Popenoe would find himself enduring punishing hardship, surviving on rotten food and barely potable water, and being stung by swarms of insects. He captured his feelings in a poem called "Wanderlust" about struggling through endless valleys and open plains: "Forward you must go / To quench the awful flames / Nor do you know / The Whither nor the Why." In a tragic incident, the first of his three wives, Dorothy Poponoe (a talented artist, archaeologist, and writer), died after eating an unripe akee fruit in Honduras (see page 296). She was only 33 years old.

He continued as a fruit hunter, venturing through the Brazilian Amazon in hopes of bringing back particularly rare tropical fruits such as the jaboticaba, a kind of glossy, glassy, grape-like purple orb that grows directly on the trunks of its trees. According to one fruit hunter I spoke with, the jaboticaba "looks like an alien embryo and tastes totally out of this world." Having successfully completed his mission, Popenoe returned to Washington, DC, where a celebratory banquet was held by Fairchild, who read aloud from his poem "The Quest of the Jaboticaba": "The men have returned, they are back from Brazil, / And the stories they tell would make your blood chill. / T'was a weird kind of fruit that they went for you see [...] Few men can do what they surely have done / Caught the jaboticaba without using a gun."

Unfortunately, as far as I can tell, no botanical watercolor painting was ever done of the jaboticaba—but David Fairchild's name comes up in conjunction with luscious paintings in the USDA's watercolor collection of papayas, cashew nuts, and fruit, as well as Deborah Griscom Passmore's glorious rendering of mangosteens (see page 309), considered the most exquisite of all tropical fruits. Documenting the findings that plant explorers brought or sent back to the US, whether through paintings or illustrations, was another responsibility of the Division of Pomology. "In addition to plant explorers, other people from all over would send in specimens to the USDA," explains Susan Fugate, head of specialist collections at the National Agricultural Library. "In order to help plant taxonomists, it was also decided that illustrations could help with identifying the different specimens."

It is noteworthy that while most of the adventurers hunting for specimens were men, those responsible for producing the paintings were often women. (Around 50 percent of the artworks, in total, were done by just three women: Passmore, Amanda Almira Newton, and Mary Daisy Arnold. Six more were key participants in the program, as were 12 men.)

It's important to remember, also, that not all of the countries whose germplasm America was seeking to extract were willing participants in the rendering up of their agricultural resources. The USDA's undertaking, in terms of plant introductions, was itself an actor in the complex legacy of colonialism—one in which countries from the global North and West have extracted materials of value from the South and East in an exploitative, non-compensatory manner. This work was done to establish the US as an internationally dominant commercial force. And while there was certainly a modicum of egalitarian intent in preserving germplasm from far-off locations, there was also undoubtedly a mercenary dimension to the endeavor. As such, the watercolor collection too, however beautiful—as part of a cataloging exercise driven by commercial and scientific interests—remains an artefact of American neoimperialism.

With all of that in mind, the Food and Agriculture Organization of the United Nations (FAO) has today ensured that the International Code of Conduct for Plant Germplasm Collecting and Transfer is followed "to promote the conservation, collection and use of plant genetic resources from their natural habitats or surroundings, in ways that respect the environment and local traditions and cultures." Doing so requires the participation of farmers, scientists, and organizations in countries where germplasm is collected so that any transfer of genetic materials is done both ethically and legally, following local customs, rules, and regulations. One of the program's goals is to avoid the sort of situations that arose in the past wherein benefits derived from plant genetic resources by local communities and farmers would accrue to other nations. The FAO's Code of Conduct also, encouragingly, promotes "the sharing of benefits derived from plant genetic resources between the donors and users of germplasm [...] by suggesting ways in which the users may pass on a share of the benefits to the donors."

That these important steps are being taken helps to deepen the context of the paintings. What makes them more than simply objects of beauty is that they document important steps already taken, while also continuing to have scientific utility. Today, genetics play a fundamental role in horticulture, but taxonomy and nomenclature remain important branches of botanical understanding. Not only have earlier efforts enabled scientists to do the sort of genetic experimentation they're undertaking today, but there are still taxonomists who refer to the paintings in their efforts to unravel the past and contextualize modern-day science.

As this book was being prepared, two news stories surfaced that showed the ongoing importance of the USDA's Pomological Watercolor Collection in the present day. Both stories involved the rediscovery of apples that had been thought to have gone extinct but which, through the diligent efforts of certain individuals and organizations, were found to still exist.

The first story involved ten varieties of "lost" apples that resurfaced as part of a collaboration between the Temperate Orchard Conservancy in Oregon and the nonprofit Lost Apple Project. Their rescue operations involve volunteer apple foragers sending in samples they have plucked from trees still growing in the grounds of abandoned homesteads or built-over orchards. To evaluate these apples, botanists at the Temperate Orchard Conservancy begin by checking to see if any of them display characteristics that align with entries in the USDA's watercolor collection. (They can't utilize DNA analyses because no genetic evaluations were ever performed.) Suspected rediscoveries such as the

14

Sary Sinap or the Butter Sweet can easily be compared against the botanical illustrations in the USDA's archive (see pages 39 and 26). Apple scientists are so adept at distinguishing identifying features that they can confirm varieties by looking at key markers, such as starry lenticles on the skin or by isolating depressions or other indentations around an apple's calyx (remnants of the blossom that remain at the base of a fruit).

The second story involved a Colorado couple's two-decade search for another ostensibly extinct apple called the Colorado Orange. Addie and Jude Schuenemeyer of the Montezuma Orchard Restoration Project had spent years documenting the more than 400 types of apples that had formerly been grown in the state. Around half of these had vanished, including the Colorado Orange, once considered an important cultivar. When they finally stumbled across the object of their pursuit, it consisted of "a nearly dead tree, a few apples dangling off its last living branch." They turned to the USDA Pomological Watercolor Collection to help substantiate their oblate, ribbed, yellow-orange rediscovery (see page 27).

The USDA's watercolor paintings and illustrations continue in their relevance—to seekers of lost apple cultivars and breeders of pink blueberries, of course—and, as Susan Fugate has expertly described them, "an invaluable source of information about the history of fruit culture in the United States." Certainly they are that, and they are a great deal more to anyone who appreciates beauty—I think of them just as I do of the visionary paintings being created in Europe during the same period: as vitamins for our eyes.

Notes

1. Germplasm is genetic material or tissue, whether seeds, stems, clippings, pollen, scions, cells, or other material containing DNA that can be used to grow new plants.

2. Phytogeography, or botanical geography, is a branch of biogeography concerned with the geographic distribution of plant species and their influence on the earth's surface.

3. cf. *The Origins of Fruits and Vegetables* by Jonathan Roberts (Universe, 2001) and *The Origin of Cultivated Plants* by Alphonse de Candolle (Kegan Paul, Trench, 1884).

4. William Henry Prestele, in 1887, was the first artist to be appointed to the staff of the USDA Pomological Division. He was assigned to make life-size watercolors of native grapes intended as illustrations for a monograph by Thomas Volney Munson, a leading authority on native grapes. The book was never printed as it would have been prohibitively expensive. Munson went on to use his text for the highly regarded book *Foundations of American Grape Culture,* which used photographs instead. Prestele's watercolors remain in the collection of the USDA.

A group of employees of the Division of Horticultural and Pomological
Investigations, photographed 7 July, 1914.

1. H. P. Gould	15. Julia Pearce	29. D. N. Shoemakeer
2. Mrs Gould	16. Emma C. Herrick	30. Ruby Ridenhower
3. R. L. Sharp	17. Grace Graham	31. Margaret Connor
4. Gus Pederson	18. Geo. M. Darrow	32. C. A. Reed
5. F. E. Bechtold	19. H. J. Ramsey	33. Mrs. Stubenrauch
6. C. P. Close	20. S. J. Dennis	34. Mabel Hiatt
7. H. C. Thompson	21. W. F. Wight	35. Bailey Stubenrauch
8. Amanda A. Newton	22. Wm Stuart	36. Ellen R. Schutt
9. Mae McWilliams	23. A. W. McKay	37. Clara E. Ballard
10. Janette Campbell	24. Geo. C. Husmann	38. H. E. Clark
11. Georgia Sturtevant	25. Chas. Dearing	39. L. B. Scott
12. Mary D. Arnold	26. Hugh Davis	40. August Maier
13. W. F. Fletcher	27. Howard Yahraus	41. Pat Marcy
14. A. V. Stuberauch	28. Alice Engle	42. S. K. Ellison

Artists of the USDA's Division of Pomology

In 1887, when the USDA's newly founded Division of Pomology set out to create a national register of fruits, photography was not yet widespread as a documentary medium. To create technically accurate illustrations, the division turned to one of the leading botanical painters of the time, William Henry Prestele. Over the next four decades, 65 more artists joined him at the Division of Pomology, including a significant number of women. This book includes watercolor paintings by 21 of these artists, namely (in descending order of number of artworks contributed): Deborah Griscom Passmore, Amanda Almira Newton, Mary Daisy Arnold, Royal Charles Steadman, James Marion Shull, Ellen Isham Schutt, Bertha Heiges, Elsie Lower, William Henry Prestele, Louis Charles Christopher Krieger, M. Strange, Harriet Thompson, Frank Muller, Roberta Cowing, Henry Van Deman, J. F. Brewer, W. L. Burn, Katherine Mayo, Eliza Swann, Charles Hopkins, and J. Sedgwick. Regrettably, little biographical information is available for most of the illustrators, but the following nine were among the most prolific.

Deborah Griscom Passmore

(1840–1911) studied at the Academy of Fine Arts in Philadelphia and in London, where she became acquainted with Marianne North's flower illustrations at Kew Gardens, inspiring her to paint wildflowers and lilies. She began her USDA career in 1892 and continued for 19 years, rising to lead the USDA staff artists and producing more than 1,500 pomological watercolors—one-fifth of the entire collection. Known for her meticulous process, Passmore sometimes used 100 washes to get the desired result. Alan Fusonie, the head of the National Agricultural Library's Special Collections in 1990, considers her "the finest example of the quality of the early USDA illustrators," and the scholar Greta Gaard cites her work as foundational ecofeminism.

Amanda Almira Newton

(c. 1860–1943) was the granddaughter of Isaac Newton, the first commissioner of the USDA, who died when she was a child. She worked at the USDA from 1896 to 1928, becoming one the most productive artists at the Division of Pomology—she painted more than 1,200 watercolors in that period. Her artworks, signed "A.A Newton," usually depict a whole fruit and half fruit in painstaking detail. She also fabricated wax models of some 300 specimens of fruits being grown or tested in the US during her career.

Mary Daisy Arnold

(c. 1873–1955) studied art in New York and began her career at the USDA in 1904, eventually becoming one of the longest-serving pomological artists—working there for 35 years and producing 1,060 watercolor paintings. In addition to the artworks, her work also involved mounting and coloring lantern slides. Outside of her USDA career, Arnold composed landscapes in other media, such as oil paint.

Royal Charles Steadman

(1875–1964) studied at the School of the Museum of Fine Arts and the Cowles Art School in Boston. He initially worked as a jewelry designer before joining the USDA in 1915, where he remained until his retirement in 1941. During that time, he illustrated almost 900 watercolors, including a series showing fruit damaged by freezing and cold storage. Additionally, he produced flower still lifes and landscapes, as well as pen-and-ink drawings. As a gift to his colleague Amanda Newton, he painted a portrait of her grandfather Isaac Newton, the first US Commissioner of Agriculture. Steadman was also a wax-fruit modeler, and he developed a patented method of strengthening wax fruit using plaster.

James Marion Shull

(1872–1948) started his career as a music and art teacher in Midwestern public schools, before joining the government as a dendrological artist for the US Forest Service in 1907. He worked for more than three decades as a botanist and illustrator for the USDA's Bureau of Plant Industry. Many of his watercolors depict infected fruit, as Shull was also a disease investigator. He also painted several early iris hybrids developed by the breeder Bruce Williamson, which prompted him to breed plants himself. He subsequently achieved recognition as an iris and daylily breeder.

Ellen Isham Schutt

(1873–1955) grew up with six older siblings in Cherrydale, Virginia, where her father owned land. At age 27, she built a large neoclassical house in the area, known as "Ellenwood," which was made entirely of concrete as protection against fire—an important feature for Schutt, who had seen a fire ravage her family home when she was a child. Schutt worked for the USDA between 1904 and 1914. In that time, she produced 700 watercolors, several of which show fruit damaged by mold and insects, and she also modeled apples and pears in wax to show the effects of long storage and packaging on the fruit.

Elsie E. Lower

(1882–1971) studied at the Corcoran School of Art, and began working at the USDA in 1908, initially drawing botanical illustrations for the yearbooks. In 1911, she married Carl Stone Pomeroy, a USDA pomologist. Two years later, the couple moved to California, where Pomeroy joined the Citrus Experiment Station, and Lower painted watercolors of the citrus industry in Riverside, a series that was exhibited throughout the US and won numerous awards. In the 1930s and 1940s, Lower traveled extensively in California. Her landscape and cityscape paintings of that period epitomize the California Scene Painting movement.

William Henry Prestele

(1838–1895) was born in Germany. His family imigrated to America in 1843, and he learned watercolor painting and lithography from his father, also a fruit and flower painter. Prestele was the first artist appointed to the Division of Pomology in 1887, initially commissioned to make life-size watercolors of native grapes to accompany a monograph by the horticulturist Thomas Volney Muson. The cost of printing the artworks was prohibitive, though, and Munson's *Foundations of American Grape Culture* was illustrated with photographs instead. Prestele's watercolors remained in the USDA collection.

Louis Charles Christopher Krieger

(1873–1940) was a botanical artist and mycologist, regarded as the finest painter of North American fungi. He began working at the USDA at the age of 18 as an assistant in the Division of Microscopy, and moved on to become an illustrator for mycologist William Gilson Farlow at Harvard University, a position he maintained for ten years. Subsequently, he worked for the USDA in California and Cuba, painting cacti and sugarcane diseases. He produced fruit watercolors only toward the end of his career in the 1930s, focusing on apples, citrus, and stone fruit.

Pomes

21

No. 97772.
Pinnacle
Arlington Farm.
Arlington No. 3087.

R. G. Steadman.
11 - 5 - '19.

The tale most often associated with apples is the creation myth of the Abrahamic religions. In the Garden of Eden, Adam and Eve know no violence, and marvelous orchards abound. They are permitted to eat from all plants but one—the tree of the knowledge of good and evil. A serpent convinces Eve to eat the forbidden fruit of the tree, and Adam joins her in doing so—the original sin. God banishes them from the Garden, and makes clear to them the dire consequences of their disobedience.

This story has inspired artists for millennia—representations of the scene are myriad. The story, as told in the Torah, the Bible, and the Quran, does not mention the temptation fruit's variety, but artworks routinely depict it as an apple. In Titian's *Adam and Eve* (c. 1550), the woman picks the golden apple from the tree as an angel watches. Here are the roots of the association, in the collective unconscious, of apples as symbols of maleficence and lust. Despite their being the most commonplace of fruits, the enduring mystique and superstition surrounding apples makes them anything but a tiresome subject.

The above notwithstanding, pears and quinces are no less important. With apples, these fruits belong to the botanic family of pomes, which encompasses fruits wherein the core is made of seeds. Stemming from the Latin *pomum* (orchard fruit), the word *pome* shares its etymology with Pomona, the goddess of fruitful abundance in Roman mythology. Besides her attribute, a pruning knife, Pomona is often portrayed with a cornucopia (horn of plenty), a large horn or horn-shaped container overflowing with fruits and flowers, emblematic of abundance, prosperity, and nourishment.

Pomes have held their place in art from classical antiquity to the present day. Should this apparent obsession seem unfathomable, looking at the fruits themselves—their cat's-eye luster—reveals reason enough. From deep red to bright yellow, earthy green to pearly pink—the rich hues are reminiscent of fall, the season of the fruits' harvesting. The slightest variation in light brings a new palette of shades and gracefully harmonic subtones to the fruits, which countless artists have sought to represent since at least the 15th century BCE, when the earliest extant still lifes, found in ancient Egyptian tombs, were painted. It has been suggested that the food depicted in these images would, in the afterlife, be real and available to the deceased.

The eye is caught by the fruits' alluring shapes. The apple's round lines are evocative of opulence and vitality; the pear's voluptuous silhouette is redolent of the female figure. This femininity is clear in Georgia O'Keeffe's *Untitled (Two Pears)* (1921), which depicts a couple of pears against a white background. The disciplined, sober mise-en-scène conceals a certain sensuality: resembling nudes on a bed, the pears become symbols and celebrations of womanhood. This correlation is one of many that show why some art historians and feminist theoreticians have regarded O'Keeffe as the originator of "female iconography" and found allegories of women's sexualities in her still lifes.

More sensory delight comes in tasting the fruit. Sweet or sour,

APPLE, PINNACLE
Nº 97772
Malus domestica
Rosslyn, Arlington County,
Virginia, USA
R. C. Steadman, 1919

23

crunchy or soft, granular or velvety—
each of the thousands of varieties of
apples, pears, and quinces possesses
unique characteristics, so even the
most fickle of palates will find one to
their liking. According to the American
naturalist and poet Henry David
Thoreau, the taste of apples differs not
only with variety but also in context.
In his 1862 article "Wild Apples,"
published in *The Atlantic*, he argues
that the fruit should be enjoyed only
outdoors, and straight from the tree,
when its aroma is at its finest:

"I frequently pluck wild apples of so
rich and spicy a flavor that I wonder
all orchardists do not get a scion from
that tree, and I fail not to bring home
my pockets full. But perchance, when
I take one out of my desk and taste it
in my chamber, I find it unexpectedly
crude—sour enough to set a squirrel's
teeth on edge and make a jay scream.
[...] The out-door air and exercise
which the walker gets give a different
tone to his palate, and he craves a
fruit which the sedentary would call
harsh and crabbed. They must be
eaten in the fields, when your system
is all aglow with exercise, when the
frosty weather nips your fingers, the
wind rattles the bare boughs."

Cydonia oblonga
Malus
Malus domestica
Pyrus calleryana
Pyrus communis
Pyrus pyrifolia

24

APPLE, CHELAN
Nº 111875
Malus domestica
Wenatchee, Chelan County,
Washington, USA
R. C. Steadman, 1931

25689
"Butter Sweet (of Pa".)
Beny. Buckman,
Farmingdale, Sangamon Co. Ill.
8/21/02
B. Heiges
9/11/02

APPLE, BUTTER SWEET OF PENNSYLVANIA
Nº 25689
Malus domestica
Farmingdale, Sangamon County,
Illinois, USA
B. Heiges, 1902

44795
"Col. Orange"
Martha Shute
Wm Bell
Canyon City, Colo.

Elsie E. Lower.
10-1-1909
12-31-1909

APPLE, COLORADO ORANGE
Nº 44795a
Malus domestica
Canon City, Fremont County,
Colorado, USA
E. E. Lower, 1909

The Colorado apple seen above, with its noticeable yellow skin and occasional red blush, was until recently thought to be an extinct variety. However, it was rediscovered in Fermont County in a historic orchard that was initially created for the prison system. The orchard is now owned by Paul Telck, who describes the fruit as being "an apple, with a unique texture and taste. It has a little bit of a citrus bite."

APPLE, ADAMS
Nº 107904
Malus domestica
Rosslyn, Arlington County,
Virginia, USA
R. C. Steadman, 1927

Regarded as a fairly dry apple, the Adams apple has a
distinct nutty and aromatic flavor similar to that of the
Victorian and Egremont Russet varieties.

39503
Alfriston Pippin
H.C.B. Colville
Missoula
Mont. Colville

Elsie E. Lower
O 6 '7
Feb. 21 - 1908

APPLE, ALFRISTON PIPPIN
Nº 39503
Malus domestica
Missoula, Missoula County,
Montana, USA
E. E. Lower, 1908

The Alfriston Pippin, thought to be the parent of the world-renowned Cox's Orange Pippin variety (see page 38), has a less-refined and more robust flavor than its offspring.

29

#18082
Grimes
from Prof Wesley Webb
Dover, Kent Co. Del.
D. G. Passmore

APPLE, GRIMES
Nº 18082
Malus domestica
Dover, Kent County,
Delaware, USA
D. G. Passmore, n.d.

No. 33885
R. I. Greening.
Immediate Storage.

No. 33884.
R. I. Greening.
Delayed Storage.
S. H. Fulton
Stuyvesant Falls. Columbia Co., N.Y.

Withdrawn 3-23-1905

Delay 2 weeks - Scald

E. I. Schutt

3/25/1905

APPLE, RHODE ISLAND GREENING
Nº 33884 & 33885
Malus domestica
Stuyvesant Falls, Columbia County,
New York, USA
E. I. Schutt, 1905

This illustration of two Rhode Island Greening apples shows the effects of delayed storage. One apple *(top)* was put into storage two weeks before the other *(bottom)*, which is visually darker in color. The Rhode Island Greening dates back to the 1650s, making it one of the oldest American varieties of *Malus domestica* known.

APPLE, ROME BEAUTY CHIMERA
Nº 111853
Malus domestica
Wenatchee, Chelan County,
Washington, USA
R. C. Steadman, 1931

32

APPLE, ROME BEAUTY
Nº 110670 & 110671
Malus domestica
Location unknown
R. C. Steadman, n.d.

The alternative name for this variety is the Second Red Rome Beauty.

APPLE, YORK
Nº 313
Malus domestica
Woodwardville, Anne Arundel County,
Maryland, USA
J. M. Shull, 1910

This illustration by J. M. Shull shows the flowering stem of a York apple tree.

#15232
Surprise
from
W. F. Reeves,
Montrose,
per   Montrose Co. Colo.
Hon. John C. Bell, M. C.

B. Heiges
1/20/98

1-18-98

APPLE, SURPRISE
№ 15232
Malus domestica
Montrose, Montrose County,
Colorado, USA
B. Heiges, 1898

The Surprise apple is distinguishable by its smallish size,
yellow skin, and pink flesh. In the early 1830s the apple was
brought from Siberia to Europe; a decade later, German
immigrants are known to have carried the variety to the US,
where it was planted in the Ohio Valley.

35625
"Pilot"
S. H. Fulton,
Grown by
W. T. Wilkinson
Richmond
Henrico Co. Va.
1-25-'06

A. A. Newton
3-12-06

APPLE, PILOT
Nº 35625
Malus domestica
Richmond,
Virginia, USA
A. A. Newton, 1906

The multipurpose Virginian Pilot apple was for decades thought to be extinct, until its rediscovery in 1989 by Tom Burford, an expert on heirloom apple varieties dedicated to reintroducing lost fruits into American culture.

No. 34048.
Old tree.

No. 34049.
Northern Spy.
Young tree
Syracuse
Onondaga Co. N.Y.
S. S. Hitchings

E. I. Schutt
April 24-1905.

APPLE, NORTHERN SPY
Nº 34048 & 34049
Malus domestica
Syracuse, Onondaga County,
New York, USA
E. I. Schutt, 1905

This illustration shows two Northern Spy apples taken from trees of different ages: a young tree *(top)* and an old tree *(bottom)*. In 2013, the US Postal Service included the Northern Spy, together with the Baldwin, Golden Delicious, and Granny Smith varieties, in a set of four stamps commemorating the historic strains.

37737
Cox's Orange Pippin
H. C. B. Colvill
Missoula
Missoula Co. Mont.

D.G. Passmore
Feb 6ᵗʰ 07
Mar 18 ° 07

APPLE, COXS ORANGE PIPPIN
Nº 37737
Malus domestica
Missoula, Missoula County,
Montana, USA
D. G. Passmore, 1907

APPLE, SARY SINAP
N° 19541
Malus domestica
Simferopol, Ukraine
D. G. Passmore, 1900

No. 56493.
Spitzenburg
B. B. Pratt, Portland, Ore.
N. Yakima
& Wash.

E. I. Schutt.
May 25 – 1912.
June 26 – 12.

Eopus.
poorly
colored.
when
picked

19 year old trees

Lot 18. Picked 10/7/11, stored 10/10/11, withdrawn about 5/10/12

APPLE, SPITZENBERG
Nº 56493
Malus domestica
Yakima, Yakima County,
Washington, USA
E. I. Schutt, 1912

Recognized as one of Thomas Jefferson's favorite varieties,
the Spitzenburg was once described by the 19th-century American
pomologist A. J. Downing as "a handsome, truly delicious apple [...]
unsurpassed as a dessert fruit." Jefferson himself planted 32
of these handsome apple trees in the South Orchard at Monticello
between 1807 and 1812. Today the apples are still considered one
of the finest varieties in production.

APPLE, DELICIOUS
Nº 55797
Malus domestica
Portland, Multnomah County,
Oregon, USA
M. D. Arnold, 1912

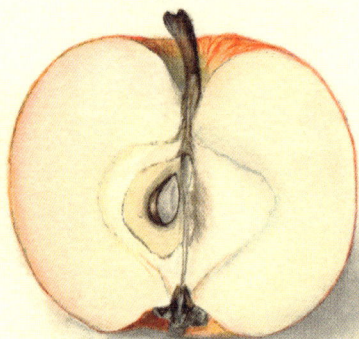

APPLE, CAGLE SEEDLING
Nº 49720
Malus domestica
Geneva, Ontario County,
New York, USA
E. E. Lower, 1911

75114 1/2
Piedmont
Valler Whatley
Crozet.
Va.

Mary D. Arnold
9-29-14
10-4-14

APPLE, PIEDMONT
Nº 75114 1/2
Malus domestica
Crozet, Albemarle County,
Virginia, USA
M. D. Arnold, 1914

34037-6
Baldwin - sod tilled

34036 7
Baldwin - tilled sod
F. A. Salisbury,
Phelps, Ontario Co.,
N. Y.
4/24/05
B. Heiges
5/10/05

APPLE, BALDWIN
N⁰ 34036 & 34037
Malus domestica
Phelps, Ontario County,
New York, USA
B. Heiges, 1905

The two Baldwin apples illustrated show the difference between one
that is tilled *(top)* and one that is sod *(bottom)*. Tillage decreases
competition of trees with sod or other crops during the early part
of the season when moisture and nitrates may be inadequate for both.
"What the Concord is among grapes, what the Bartlett has been among
pears, the Baldwin is among apples," announced the *New England
Farmer* in 1885, ranking the Baldwin among the great varieties of fruits.

44

APPLE, BEN DAVIS × ESOPUS
Nº 55078
Malus domestica
Geneva, Ontario County,
New York, USA
E. I. Schutt, 1912

The seedling of this apple was a cross between the Ben Davis and Esopus varieties. The Ben Davis apple is characterized by its medium size and waxy, bright yellow skin that is often mottled with dark and bright red blushing. In 1910 a bulletin stated that these Southern-grown apples were "generally more juicy and of notably better quality" than their Northern-grown counterparts, such as the Esopus.

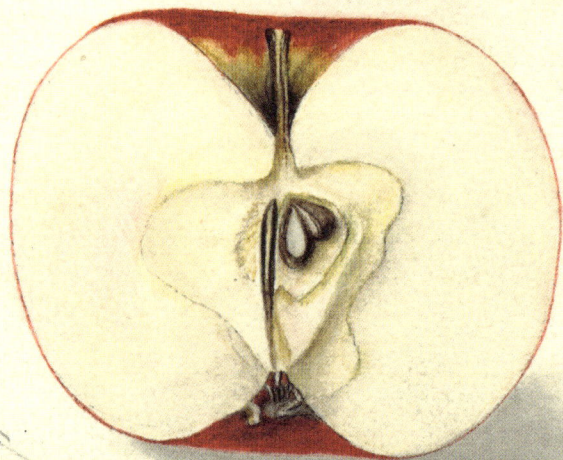

APPLE, SAN JACINTO
Nº 17689a
Malus domestica
Pilot Point, Denton County,
Texas, USA
D. G. Passmore, 1899

This watercolor illustration was produced as a mock-up for the *Yearbook of Agriculture 1911*.

The USDA, which was established in 1862, began the production of its annual yearbooks in 1894. Up until that point the department had been issuing a single volume of its own reports for governmental records. This single volume was split in two: one book was designed for business and executive matters that were necessary to be submitted to the President and Congress, and the second, the yearbooks, contained reports from different bureau divisions and selected papers that were accompanied by illustrations.

The yearbooks contained a collection of articles on current agriculture research and studies, plus statistical tables. The illustrations that were chosen to be reproduced as lithographs in each volume depict the fruits mentioned in the articles. Each illustration in the yearbooks has a set format of annotation, informative in intention, which adds accidental beauty. At the top left of the page in neat, typewritten sans serif text, appears "Yearbook U.S. Dept. of Agriculture" and the year. Opposite, in the right-hand corner, in small capitals appears "PLATE," followed by its Roman numeral. At the bottom left is the sample number of the fruit illustrated, the variety's name, and who the sample was sent by and from where. At the bottom right is the signature of the illustrator and the date of the image's original creation. Beneath these, in the center of the page, appears the variety in capitals, and in the right margin is the lithograph printer's name and address.

Studies of apple twigs, buds and foliage.
(top) APPLE, SWEET BOUGH, Nº 82819, *Malus domestica*, South Haven, Van Buren County, Michigan, USA. R. C. Steadman, 1919. (bottom) APPLE, HYSLOP, Nº 9201919, *Malus domestica*, South Haven, Van Buren County, Michigan, USA. R. C. Steadman, 1919.

Decarie.
Exp. Station.
So. Haven, Mich.

R. C. Steadman.
9 - 13 - '19.

APPLE, DECARIE
N° 91319
Malus domestica
South Haven, Van Buren County,
Michigan, USA
R. C. Steadman, 1919

10814
"#64 - Arkansas Black"
John S. Stinson
Fayetteville
Ark

D. G. Passmore
11/1/95

APPLE, ARKANSAS BLACK
Nº 10814
Malus domestica
Fayetteville, Washington County,
Arkansas, USA
D. G. Passmore, 1895

Noted for its delicious balance of sweetness and bitterness,
the Arkansas Black is recognized as being one of the top 10
varieties for making apple juice.

No. 99704
Arkansas Black.
Arlington Farm.

R. G. Steadman
1 17 '21.

APPLE, ARKANSAS BLACK
Nº 99704
Malus domestica
Rosslyn, Arlington County,
Virginia, USA
R. C. Steadman, 1921

J. M. Shull studies of decay stages of apples (*Malus domestica*).
(top left) YELLOW NEWTON PIPPIN, Nº 801, Covesville, Albemarle County, Virginia, USA, 1914.
Pear blight on a nearly grown fruit, thought to be a Yellow Newtown Pippin. This sample carried an
abundance of germs, and was exuding gum and rapidly discoloring clear to the margins. *(top right)*
BEN DAVIS, Nº 1069, Vienna, Fairfax County, Virginia, USA, 1918. This illustration shows both
sides and a section of the same fruit. *(bottom left)* RED PEARMAIN, Nº 299, Pasadena, Los
Angeles County, California, USA, 1910. (a) Early stage of core decay and (b) more advanced decay.
(bottom right) APPLE, ROME, Nº 1628, Wenatchee, Chelan County, Washington, USA, 1935.
A note from a letter dated 2 April 1936 states this apple is the same as specimen Nº 1626.

Fire blight or *Erwinia amylovora* is a common, destructive, and contagious bacterium found in apples, pears, and other members of the Rosaceae family. It causes blackening of leaves, wilting of blossoms, and reddish water-soaked lesions of the bark. These lesions, on warm days, ooze an orange-brown liquid that runs down the living bark, attacking the larger limbs and trunk on its way.

Untreated, blight has been known to cause large-scale destruction of entire orchards and native fruit varieties within a single growing season.

Originating in North America, fire blight has now spread to many parts of the world. It is listed as a quarantine disease in Europe. Due to trade restrictions, it has never taken hold in Australia.

Blight is a deadly disease for plants, and hugely damaging for farmers and economies. The bacterium can be controlled by pruning out and burning the infected areas, with the removal of secondary late blossom being advised.

PEAR, BARTLETT SECKEL × BARTLETT   This pear is a cross between a Bartlett and a Bartlett Seckel.
N° 112444
Pyrus communis
South Haven, Van Buren County,
Michigan, USA
M. D. Arnold, 1932

PEAR, FORELLA
Nº 52450
Pyrus communis
Santa Clara, Santa Clara County,
California, USA
M. D. Arnold, 1911

The Forella (or Forelle) pear is thought to have originated in northern Saxony, Germany, around the 1600s. The variety gets its name from the German word for "trout" due to its brilliant red lenticels, which are similar to the colors seen on a rainbow trout.

PEAR, BELLE ANGEVINE
Nº 20898
Pyrus communis
Fleury-sous-Meudon,
Île-de-France, France
D. G. Passmore, 1900

The original notes for this and the following illustration have
been corrected from Fleury-Meudon to Fleury-sous-Meudon.

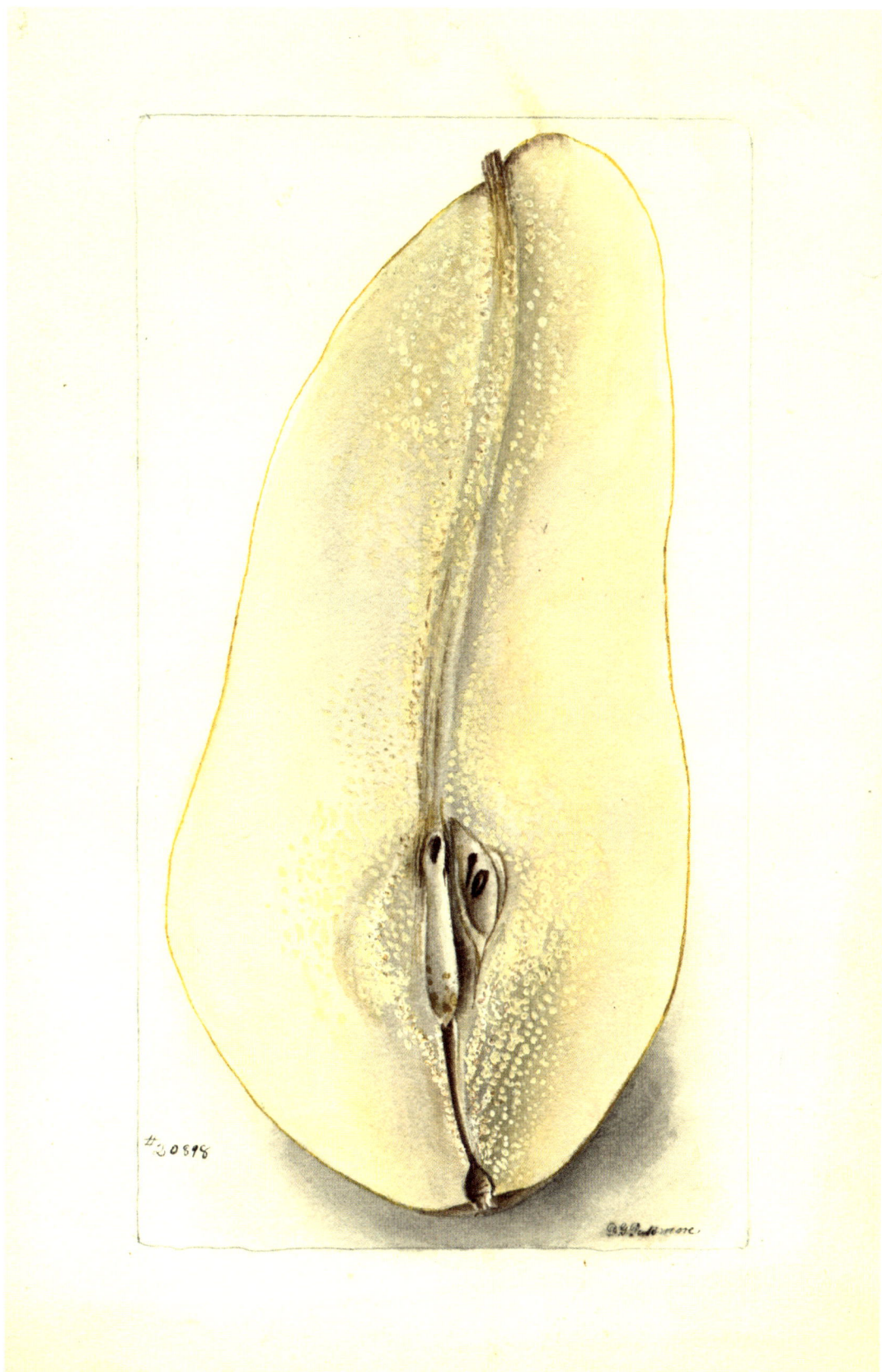

PEAR, BELLE ANGEVINE
Nº 20898a
Pyrus communis
Fleury-sous-Meudon,
Île-de-France, France
D. G. Passmore, 1900

Belle Angevine pears are noted for their beauty, brilliant color, and large, attractive shape. However, despite its appearance, the pear is in fact less than desirable for its flavor.

20936
Konig Karl von Wurtemberg
Austria
G. B. Brackett
Paris Exp. France.

D. G. Passmore
12.8.1900

PEAR, KONIG KARL VON WURTTEMBERG
Nº 20936
Pyrus communis
Austria
D. G. Passmore, 1900

The specimen shown above and in the following illustration was received from G. B. Brackett on return from the Paris Exposition of 1900, France.

20936
Konig Karl von Wurtemberg-Austria
G. B. Brackett
Paris Exp. France

J. G. Passmore
14.8.1900

PEAR, KONIG KARL VON WURTTEMBERG
Nº 20936a
Pyrus communis
Austria
D. G. Passmore, 1900

No.61606.
Bosc.
K. B. Lewis. Portland. Oreg.
Hollywood. Orchard. Medford Oreg.
Loose Soil. Lot A13. Immediate Stor. 32°
Picked 9-12-'12.
Immediate 32° storage; first inspection

E.J.Schutt
12-9-'12
12-13-'12.

PEAR, BOSC
Nº 61606
Pyrus communis
Medford, Jackson County,
Oregon, USA
E. I. Schutt, 1912

This sample of a Bosc pear was grown in loose soil and
later picked on 9 September 1912, from Lot A13. It was
immediately placed into storage at 32°F.

60

No. 46726.
"Bosc"
Bear Creek Orchards.
Medford, Jackson Co.,
Oregon.
Stored at Merchants Ref. Co. Jersey City N.J. Oct. 22 '09. at 32°
Removed. April 4 '10 -

E. I. Schutt
Apr. 13-10
" 15 10

PEAR, BOSC
Nº 46726
Pyrus communis
Medford, Jackson County,
Oregon, USA
E. I. Schutt, 1910

This illustration shows a firm Bosc pear *(top)* and the same pear with mold on the stem and shriveled skin *(bottom)*. This pear was affected by delayed storage of five and a half months: it was stored at 32°F at the Merchant Refrigerator Company in New Jersey, from where it was removed on 4 April 1910 and kept in a warm office until 3 October the same year.

58663 a.
Bosc
"Loose Soil."
A.C. Allen's Orchard
Medford Oreg.   Picked Sept 12—   Recd Sept 19 12
Lot A13   Placed in cold storage on arrival &
         held until painted. Cut 10/4
                                    E.J. Schutt.
                                    Oct 3-1912.

PEAR, BOSC
Nº 58663a
Pyrus communis
Medford, Jackson County,
Oregon, USA
E. I Schutt, 1912

This Bosc pear was grown in loose soil and was picked on
12 September 1912, from Lot A13. It was then placed in
cold storage on arrival to E. I. Schutt, and cut in half on
4 October 1912.

PEAR, KIEFFER
Nº 23162c
Pyrus communis
Woodwardville, Anne Arundel County,
Maryland, USA
B. Heiges, 1901

This Kieffer 3rd Yellow pear was picked on 21 October 1901
and stored on 22 October at 36°F.

26055
Bartlett Select
S. H. Fulton
Barker Niagara Co N.Y.

D. G. Passmore

"Select" Bartlett - as shipped from Barker N.Y.
to London, Sept. 13, from New York

PEAR, BARTLETT SELECT
Nº 26055
Pyrus communis
Barker, Niagara County,
New York, USA
D. G. Passmore, n.d.

D. G. Passmore received this Bartlett Select pear from
S. H. Fulton. It had come originally from Baker, New York,
and been held in cold storage until 25 September
when the painting was made.

872

PEAR, KIEFFER
Nº 23781
Pyrus communis
Woodwardville, Anne Arundel County,
Maryland, USA
D. G. Passmore, 1901

This specimen was picked on 21 October 1901 and
immediately wrapped in parchment and stored the day after
at 36°F for eight weeks. It was withdrawn from storage on 14
December 1901.

No. 94081
"Champion"
O. M. Taylor.
Geneva Exp. Sta.
Geneva, N. Y.

R. G. Steadman.
1-9-'18
10-18-'17

QUINCE, CHAMPION
Nº 94081
Cydonia oblonga
Geneva, Ontario County,
New York, USA
R. C. Steadman, 1918

This specimen was received from the New York State Agricultural Experiment Station, Geneva, from the Foreman in Horticulture, O. M. Taylor.

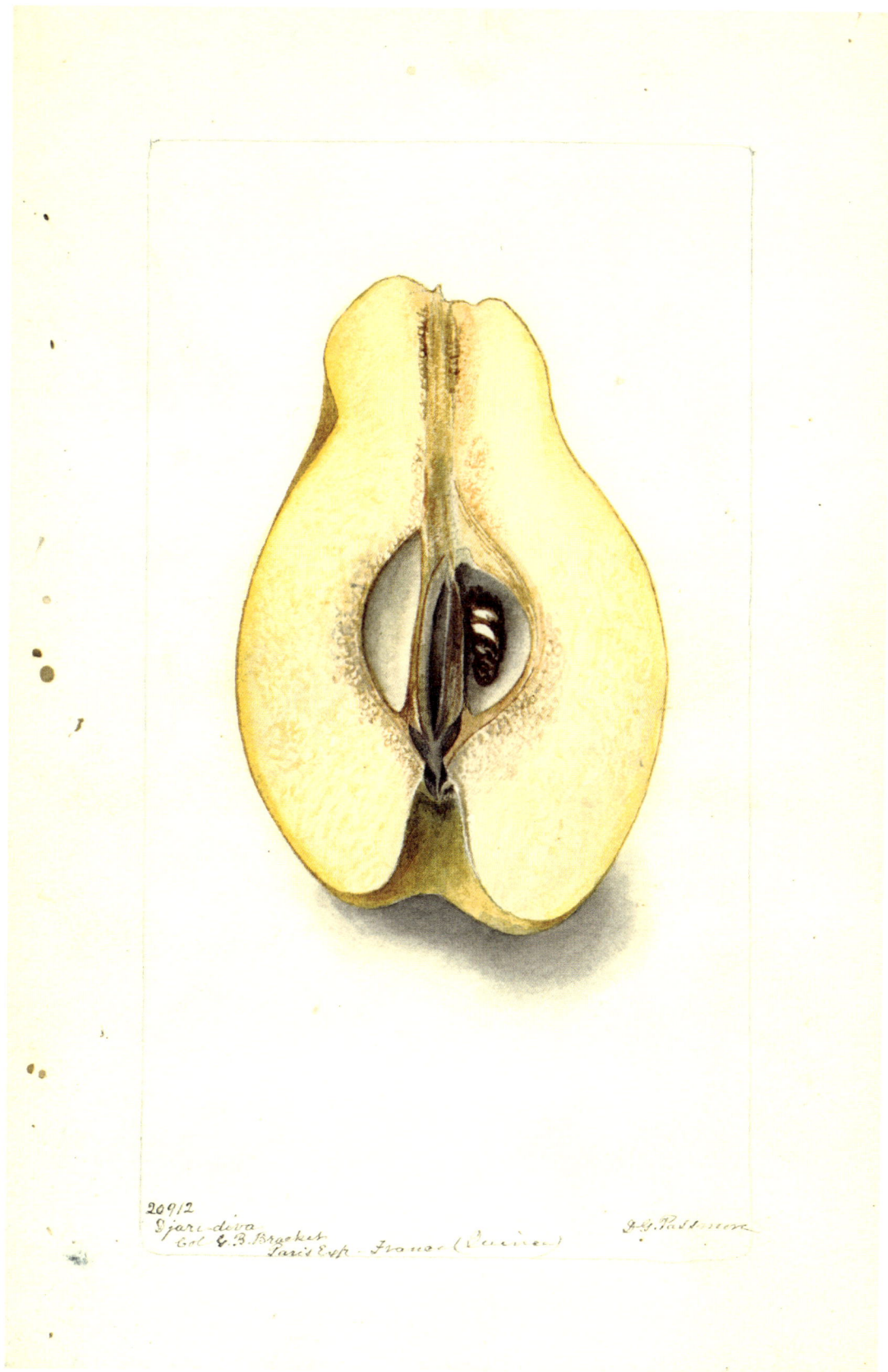

QUINCE, DJARE DIVA
Nº 20912
Cydonia oblonga
France
D. G. Passmore, n.d.

This specimen was received from G. B. Brackett on return
from the Paris Exposition of 1900, France.

PEARS
Nº 125 & 263
Pyrus communis
Caucasus
Artist unknown, n.d.

The specimens above and in the following illustration are wild pears from the Caucasus. The varieties of pears native to the Caucasus have coarse flesh that is largely sweet in flavor.

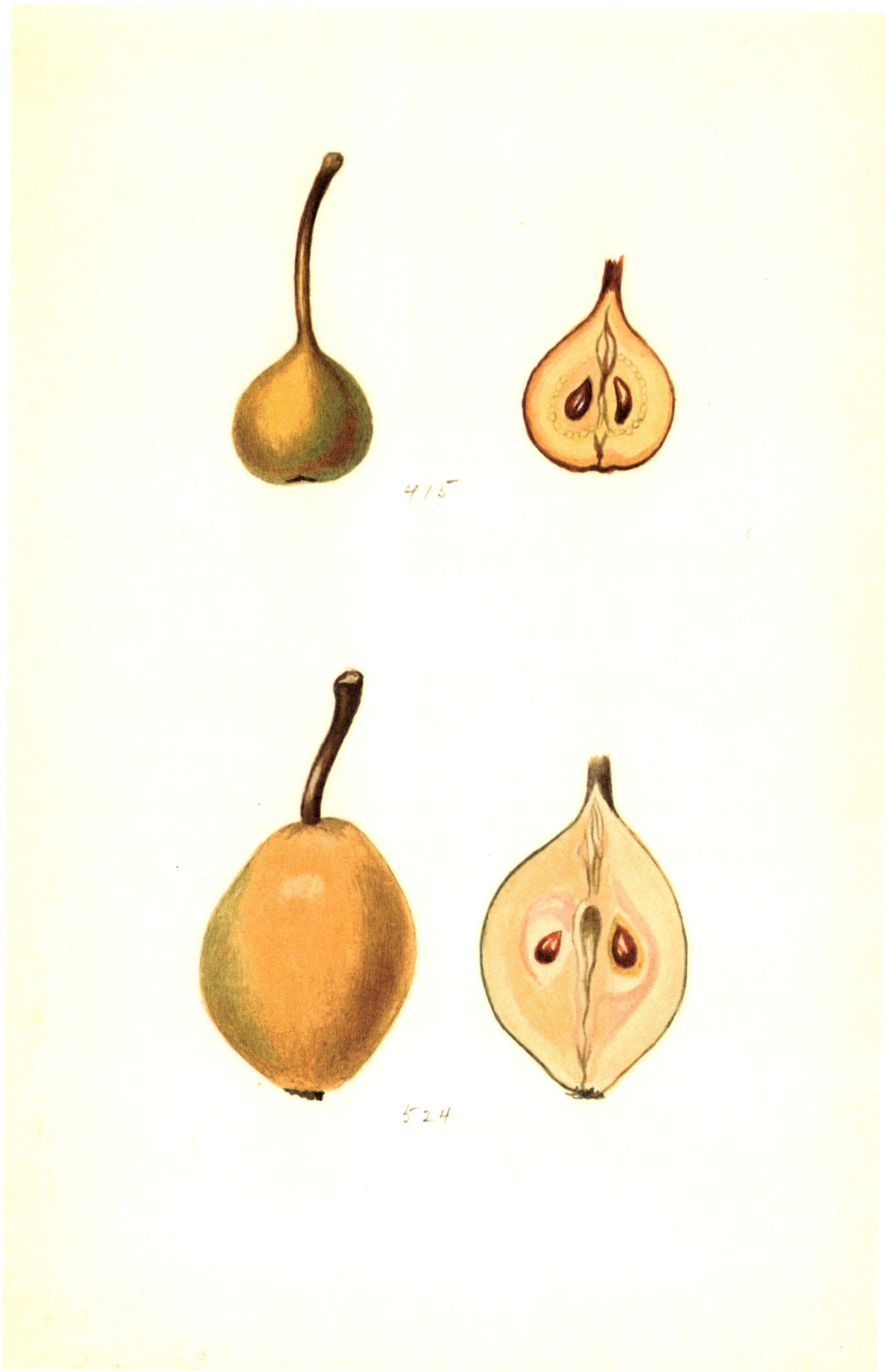

PEARS
Nº 415a & 524
Pyrus communis
Caucasus
Artist unknown, n.d.

No 57291
yellow Siberian
Exp. Sta.
College Park.
Maryland.

E. I. Schutt.
Aug 6 - 1912.
" 6 - 1912.

CRAB APPLE, YELLOW SIBERIAN
N° 57291
Malus
College Park, Prince Georges County,
Maryland, USA
E. I. Schutt, 1912

The yellow Siberian crab apple has many uses beyond the culinary world, for example the trees that produce this variety are planted by farmers as windbreaks to provide cover and food for local wildlife, such as deer and birds. The wood of the tree is also prized for its ornamental properties.

CRAB APPLE, SEPTEMBER CRAB
Nº 22646
Malus
Sheridan, Chautaugua County,
New York, USA
B. Heiges, 1902

CRAB APPLE, MONTREAL
N° 57301
Malus
College Park, Prince Georges County,
Maryland, USA
M. D. Arnold, 1912

72

No. 34876
"bathead" "Cherry Crab"
Jacob R. Payne   G. B. Brackett
Washington leafless   U.S.A.
Washington   E. I. Schutt
                          Aug 3. 1905.

CRAB APPLE, CHERRY CRAB
Nº 34376
Malus
USA
E. I. Schutt, 1905

74

R. C. Steadman
11 – 21 – '21.

No. 100496
Pyrus Calleryana, from
Arnold Arboratum .

CALLERY PEAR
Nº 100496
Pyrus calleryana
Brookline, Norfolk County,
Massachusetts, USA
R. C. Steadman, 1921

The Callery pear is commonly planted for its ornamental
value. They also produce an abundance of fruits which get
taken by birds that go on to spread the seeds of the plant in
their droppings around the local area.

105726

Japanese Pear,
L. K. Clark
Orange Va.

M. D. Arnold

ASIAN PEAR
№ 105726
Pyrus pyrifolia
Orange, Orange County,
Virginia, USA
M. D. Arnold, n.d.

Also known as the Japanese pear, as noted by L. K. Clark
(associate professor at the Indiana Veterinary Clinical
Sciences and Veterinary Teaching Hospital).

Citrus

No. 46199
America Wonder
N. B. White.
Norwood

E. J. Schutt
Jan 19-'10
"   22-10.

Z esty, intense, tangy, sweet, bitter, juicy, flamboyant: citruses demand vivid description. As a great many recollections of first chancing upon citrus fruits make clear, oranges, lemons, grapefruits, or limes tend to excite neophytes. Such an encounter is recorded by the eminent Danish writer of fairy tales, Hans Christian Andersen, who, on an expedition to Italy in 1833, found himself spellbound by the vibrant sight and scent of citrus groves—a reaction shared by many northerners who traveled to Mediterranean countries at the time. "Just imagine the beautiful ocean and entire forests with oranges and lemons," he wrote in a letter to a friend, "My God, my God! How unfairly we are treated in the north; here, here is Paradise."

While the fruits continue to put many in mind of the sun-soaked Mediterranean, their origin lies much further east. Citruses are native to South Asia, and their history, as with that of many foods and spices, is intrinsically linked to the spread of civilization and to colonialism.

Oranges are first mentioned in Chinese literature in 314 BCE, and appear widely in the art of the Song Dynasty of 11th-century China. Su Shi, the region's then most accomplished polymath, alludes to them in a poem, "For Liu Jingwen" (which in turn inspired a silk painting by Zhao Lingrang, *Yellow Oranges and Green Tangerines*):

> [...]
> You must remember,
> the best scenery of the year,
> Is exactly now,

when oranges turn yellow and tangerines green.

An array of citrus species spread to India, the Arab world, and Europe, along the former incense trade route. Although oranges can be discerned on the table in Leonardo da Vinci's *The Last Supper* (c. 1498), orange cultivation is thought to have begun in the Middle East only in the ninth century, making the renowned painting anachronistic. But this inclusion is understandable, as oranges began to arrive in Europe from the east during the Renaissance. They were pictured in many artworks of the era, and it was during the same period that "orange" entered Western languages as a color—prior to the fruit's arrival in Europe, the shade was simply referred to as "yellow-red," or sometimes just "red." Despite the orange being the only fruit to have given its name to a color, oranges can be green and perfectly ripe: the hue depends not on ripeness but on the temperature of the area in which it is grown. In milder climes, the green skin turns orange in autumn because the chlorophyll disappears as the weather cools, in a phenomenon akin to the browning of tree leaves. In tropical areas, where the weather is hot year round, orange skins stay green.

At last, citruses made their voyage to the Americas, where they became widely used in characteristically American beverages, from orange juice concentrate and cocktails to lemonade and sodas. In the 1960s, when the popularity of such drinks was burgeoning worldwide, the *New Yorker* journalist John McPhee was commissioned to write a short magazine article about oranges. He encountered so much interesting trivia that he wrote a book on the subject. In the humbly titled *Oranges*, we thus learn that in 1945 the

LEMON, AMERICAN WONDER
Nº 46199
Citrus limon
Norwood, Norfolk County,
Massachusetts, USA
E. I. Schutt, 1910

US Army ordered 500,000 pounds of powdered orange juice from the newly established Florida Foods Corporation, but the war ended before the cargo was shipped. In the years that followed, commercial concentrate in the form of frozen cans became widely popular. Although concentrate might seem slightly old-fashioned, 95 percent of the oranges grown in the Sunshine State are still used for juice, and the Florida Foods Corporation continues to trade globally under the Minute Maid name.

Postwar prosperity brought consumerism, and with it the golden age of advertising posters in all their bright colors and sharp graphics—an aesthetic quickly adopted in pop art. Ubiquitous in advertisements, citruses became artistic and commercial icons, accompanying every small daily treat: a slice of lemon boosting the taste of a cola, a glass of orange juice bringing happiness to the family, lemon zest enhancing the aroma of cheesecakes and other desserts, lime twists giving martinis the perfect bite. Symbols of health, sunshine, and pleasure—there is never a dull moment with citruses.

Citroncirus webberi
Citrus aurantiifolia
Citrus aurantium
Citrus citrofortunella
Citrus grandis
Citrus limon
Citrus nobilis
Citrus medica
Citrus paradisi
Citrus reticulata
Citrus sinensis
Citrus unshiu
Fortunella

57351
ow Leaf "Valencia-
Sport
L. B. Scott,
Corona,
Calif.

A. A. Newton.
8-8-'12
8-12-'12

sporting limb on standard tree."
Tree 1, row 92, plot 22 ($\frac{22}{92}$)

ORANGE, VALENCIA
Nº 57351
Citrus sinensis
Corona, Riverside County,
California, USA
A. A. Newton, 1912

This specimen of Valencia orange, alternatively named
Willow Leaf, was taken from a sporting limb on a standard
tree at Plot 22, Row 92, Tree 1. Despite its name, the
Valencia orange was actually first developed in the US for the
production of orange juice. It was named after the Spanish
city because of the abundance of orange trees and citrus
fruits that grow within its streets.

35724
Thornton 2
Dr. H. J. Hibber
Mr. Thornton
Orlando
Orange Co. Fla.

O. S. Passmore
2.16.06
2.23.06
Pomelo + Tangerine

GRAPEFRUIT, THORNTON Nº 2   Possibly a tangerine, not a grapefruit.
Nº 35724
Citrus paradisi
Orlando, Orange Country,
Florida, USA
D. G. Passmore, 1906

Orange Pomelo
A. L. Duncan
Dunedin Hillsboro Co
#8335   Rcd 12/17/94   Fla

D. G. Passmore

GRAPEFRUIT, ORANGE POMELO
№ 8335
Citrus paradisi
Dunedin, Pinellas Country,
Florida, USA
D. G. Passmore, 1894

"Pomelo" was historically a word used to describe a grape-fruit and has only recently been corrected to describe a shaddock fruit. Traditionally in China the leaves and the fruit's rind are boiled together to be used in the ritual cleansing of the body against evil spirits.

83

Pomo d' Adams

Citron Myers Lee Co. Fla

J. J. Eyre

#5787

G. G. Passmore

nov 15 – 1893

CITRON, POMO D'ADAMS
Nº 5787
Citrus medica
Fort Myers, Lee County,
Florida, USA
D. G. Passmore, 1893

84

No. 40291
Citron.
David Fairchild
F. N. Bessey
Miami
Dade Co, Fla.

E. I. Schutt
Jan 23 - 08.
25 - 08.

CITRON
Nº 40291
Citrus medica
Miami, Dade County,
Florida, USA
E. I. Schutt, 1908

#11407

D. G. Passmore

Los Angeles Chamber of Commerce,
Los Angeles, Cal.
Los Angeles Co.

2-18-96

CITRON, CITRON OF COMMERCE
№ 11407
Citrus medica
Los Angeles, Los Angeles County,
California, USA
D. G. Passmore, 1896

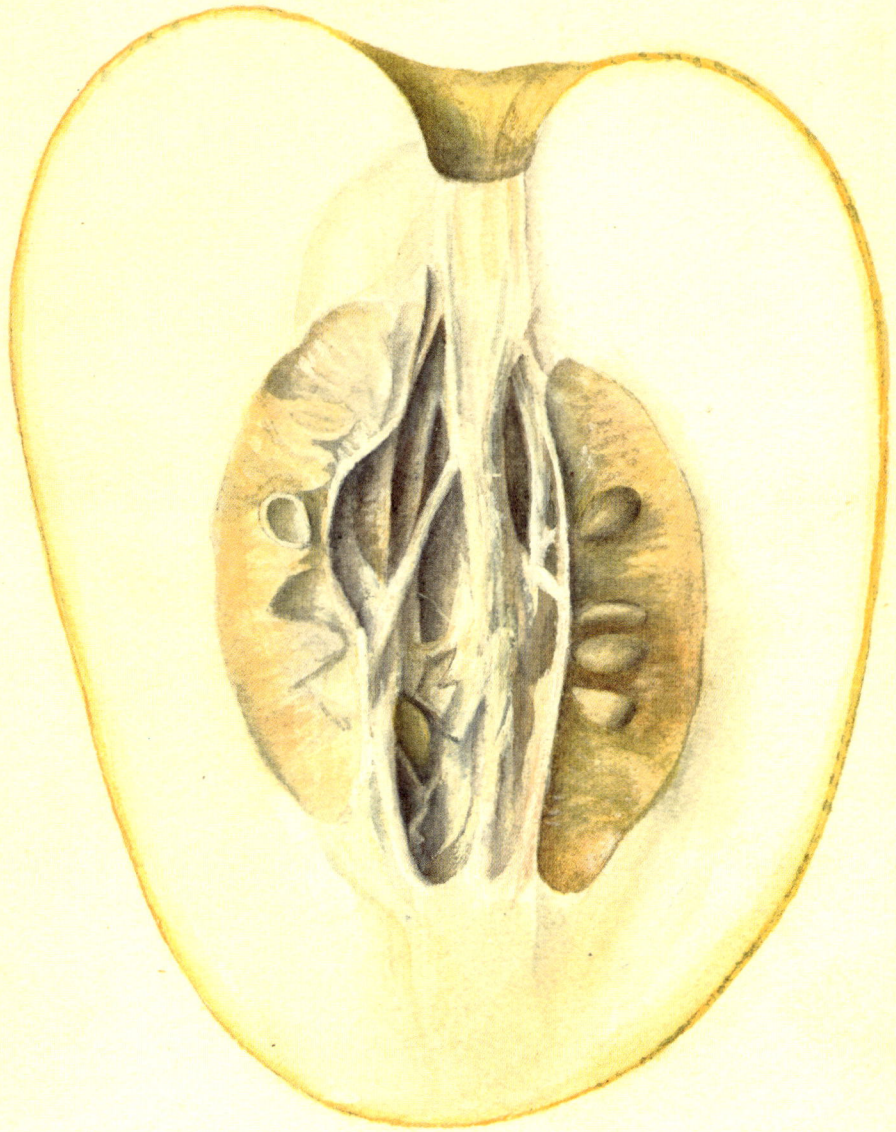

#11407
"Citron of Commerce"
from Los Angeles Chamber of Commerce
Los Angeles, Calif

D. G. Passmore

CITRON, CITRON OF COMMERCE
Nº 11407a
Citrus medica
Los Angeles, Los Angeles County,
California, USA
D. G. Passmore, 1896

Studies of grapefruit (*Citrus paradisi*) twigs and leaves.
(top) Nº 928, Coden, Mobile County, Alabama, USA. J. M. Shull, 1916. This illustration shows canker on twigs as collected on 4 May 1916 by American botanist C. H. Hasse.
(bottom) Nº 1471, Narcoossee, Osceola County, Florida, USA. J. M. Shull, 1916.

GRAPEFRUIT
№ 330
Citrus paradisi
Palmetto, Manatee County,
Florida, USA
J. M. Shull, 1910

This specimen was collected by M. B. Waite, pathologist in charge at the Fruit Disease Investigation Center, USDA.

Yearbook U. S. Dept. of Agriculture, 1905.

PLATE LIV.

No. 37437
772
Prof. H. J. Webber
agric. Dept.
Wash. D. C.

E. J. Schutt.
Nov. 19 — 1906.

Citra.

CITRANGE
N° 37437
Citroncirus webberi
Washington, DC, USA
E. I. Schutt, 1906

This watercolor is a mock-up illustration for the *Yearbook of Agriculture 1906*. Originally it was noted that this was citrus hybrid No. 772.

#61874.
Pomelo x Tangerine.
Webers - No 1311 -
Sub. Trop. Introduction Ground Miami Fla.

E. J. Schutt
Jan 4 - 13
" 9 - 13

Tangelo

TANGELO
Nº 61874
Citrus aurantium
Miami, Dade County,
Florida, USA
E. I. Schutt, 1913

Pomelo and tangerine hybrid, Webers No. 1311.

No. 96625
Marsh.
J. E. Cutler
Riverside, Cal.

R. G. Steadman.
1 – 17 – '19
12 – 30 – '18

GRAPEFRUIT, MARSH
Nº 96625
Citrus paradisi
Riverside, Riverside County,
California, USA
R. C. Steadman, 1919

No. 96625
Marsh.
J. E. Cutler
Riverside, Cal.

R. C. Steadman.
1 - 16 - '19
12 - 30 - '18

GRAPEFRUIT, MARSH
№ 96625a
Citrus paradisi
Riverside, Riverside County,
California, USA
R. C. Steadman, 1919

GRAPEFRUIT, № 1474
№ 46773a
Citrus paradisi
Florence Villa, Tampa, Hillsborough County,
Florida, USA
A. A. Newton, 1910

94

N.o. 98352.
April 20, 1920.

R. G. Steadman.
4-28-'20.

GRAPEFRUIT
Nº 98352a
Citrus paradisi
Location unknown
R. C. Steadman, 1920

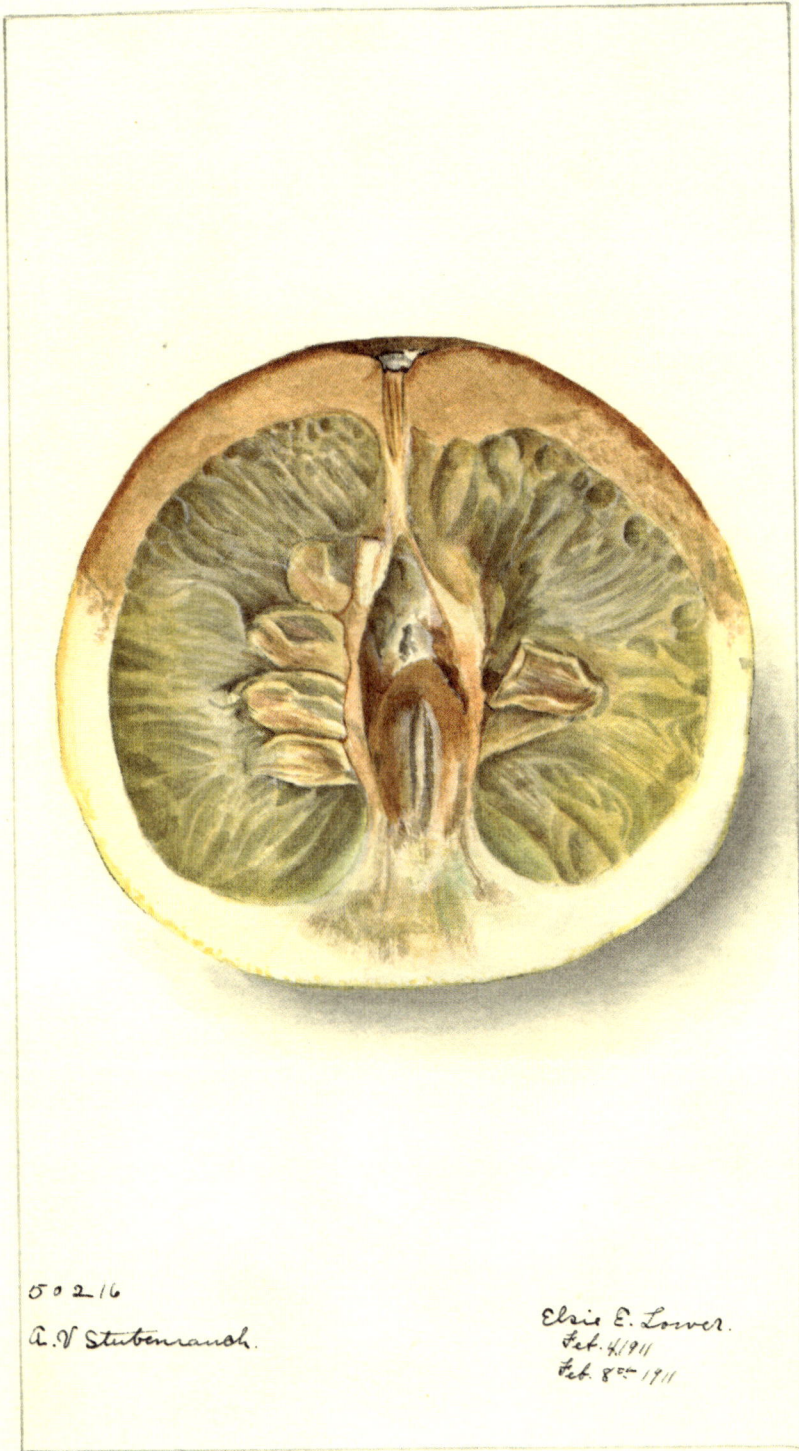

50216
a. V Stubenrauch.

Elsie E. Lower.
Feb. 4 1911
Feb. 8th 1911

GRAPEFRUIT, POMELO
N° 50216a
Citrus paradisi
Florida, USA
E. E. Lower, 1911

No 61317.
Pomelo. (pink fleshed)
John Parrish.
Parrish. Fla.
Ripens in March.

E. I. Schutt.
Nov 25-12.

2 specimens - 1 rec'd 11-23- 1 rec'd 11-25
Tree probably about 15 yrs old + 10 ft high.

GRAPEFRUIT, PINK FLESHED
Nº 61317
Citrus paradisi
Parrish, Manatee County,
Florida, USA
E. I. Schutt, 1912

This specimen was taken from a tree that was estimated to be 15 years old, 10 feet high, and ripened in March.

GRAPEFRUIT
Nº 701
Citrus paradisi
Orlando, Orange County,
Florida, USA
J. M. Shull, 1913

98

Common Fla, Grape fruit
Tree 4, Row 40
Picked Aug. 25, and held in storage
Onedora Grove
Fla.

A. A. Newton
9-4-1919

GRAPEFRUIT
Nº 941919a
Citrus paradisi
Florida, USA
A. A. Newton, 1919

This common Florida grapefruit was picked on 25 August 1919, from Tree 4, Row 40, and held in storage until it was painted.

46282
Chinese Shaddock
W. T. Swingle
Wolfskill Ranch
Winters, Yolo Co. Calif.

D. G. Passmore
2.3.1910
2.8.1910

PUMMELO, CHINESE SHADDOCK
Nº 46282a
Citrus grandis
Winters, Yolo County,
California, USA
D. G. Passmore, 1910

40364
Chinese Pomelo
W. T. Swingle
Tucson,
Ariz.

A. A. Newton
2-10-08
2-17-08

PUMMELO, CHINESE
Nº 40364
Citrus grandis
Tucson, Pima County,
Arizona, USA
A. A. Newton, 1908

The original artwork states that this is a pomelo rather than a pummelo.

No. 96570
Sampson Tangelo.
Frank Savage.
Eustis, Fla.

R. C. Steadman.
12-21-'18
11-30-'18

TANGELO, SAMPSON
Nº 96570
Citrus aurantium
Eustis, Lake County,
Florida, USA
R. C. Steadman, 1918

CITRANGES, CARNAGIE
Nº 35394
Citroncirus webberi
Marksville, Louisiana, USA
A. A. Newton, 1905

This specimen is a cross between *Citrus trifoliate* and a Boones Early from Avoyelles Parish, Louisiana.

45822
"Nagami"
La. Exp. Station
Baton Roug

Elsie E. Lower
11-22-'09
12- 1 -'09

KUMQUAT, NAGAMI
Nº 45822
Fortunella
Baton Rouge, Louisiana, USA
E. E. Lower, 1909

The Nagami is one of the most common varieties of
kumquats grown, due to its hardiness and productiveness.
During the Chinese or Lunar New Year, this variety of
kumquat is frequently given as a gift and used for decoration
in people's homes.

KUMQUAT
Nº 19134
Fortunella
Monrovia, Los Angeles County,
California, USA
D. G. Passmore, 1900

87039
Tree 1-29-8
C. S. Pomeroy
Corona
Calif.

LEMON
Nº 87039a
Citrus limon
Corona, Riverside County,
California, USA
A. A. Newton, 1916

This specimen is noted as being an odd shape when it was taken from Tree 1-29-8.

C 90872
"Etrog"
S. Island
Corfu, Greece
New York,
N.Y

A. A. Newton
10 - 1916
10 - 14 - 1916

LEMON, ETROG
Nº 90872
Citrus limon
Corfu, Ionian Islands, Greece
A. A. Newton, 1916

The etrog, alongside pomelos, mandarins, and papedas, is one of the four "founding fathers" of citrus fruits—meaning that the lemon is in fact a type of etrog. It is also said that the etrog is the "fruit of the Godly tree" as written about in the book of Genesis in the Old Testament.

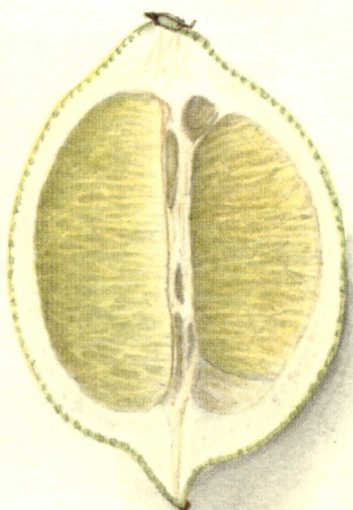

No 60939.
~~Official~~ Eureka.
A. D. Shamel.
Chase Plantation
Corona Calif.
Tree 44.   SepNov. 2-'12.

E. I. Schutt.
Nov. 8 - '12.
Nov. 14 - '12.

Photographed   11-9-12.
In green fruit of this pick, 58 smooth, 3 corrugated
evidently a limb sport.

LEMON, EUREKA
Nº 60939
Citrus limon
Corona, Riverside County,
California, USA
E. I. Schutt, 1912

This illustration shows a fruit in the green stage of ripening. From this pick, 58 were smooth, and three were corrugated and eventually developed limb sports. This specimen, picked from Tree 44, was sent by A. D. Shamel on 11 November 1912. The Eureka variety of lemon is the most widely cultivated across the globe and is commercially produced in areas of South Africa, Israel, Australia, and Argentina. Within the US, California is currently the leading domestic supplier of the fruit.

No 60939.
Typical Eureka ms.
Roughly corrugated type in same tree
at Shamel -
Chase Plantation. Tree 44.
Corona Calif. first Nov 2-12.

E. I. Schutt.
Nov 8- '12
Nov 13- 12.

Photographed 11-9-12.
On this tree in green fruit of this pick 58 smooth,
3 corrugated, evidently a limb sport.

LEMON, EUREKA
Nº 60939a
Citrus limon
Corona, Riverside County,
California, USA
E. I. Schutt, 1912

This illustration shows a typical Eureka of the rough
corrugated type taken from the same tree as specimen
No. 60939. Sent to E. I. Schutt on 11 November 1912,
painted on the 14th, and photographed on the 19th.

LEMON, MEYER
Nº 107326
Citrus limon
Oroville, Butte County,
California, USA
R. C. Steadman, 1926

The Meyer lemon is somewhere between deep yellow and yellow-orange in color. Its rounder shape and smoother skin also set it apart from other commercial varieties. It has much sweeter, less acidic juice than regular lemons. It is prized by home cooks and chefs, including Martha Stewart, who popularized the variety through dozens of recipes, such as Meyer lemon and coconut layer cake.

They were first imported from China to the United States by agricultural explorer Frank N. Meyer in 1908. Meyer first noticed the variety, with its glossy green leaves and dangling yellow fruit, outside the homes of the better-off, where, he learned, they were grown as ornamental plants.

Originating in Fengtai, now a district of Beijing, the fruit is believed by many botanists to be a cross between a lemon and a mandarin orange. If you were to buy a Meyer lemon tree now, though, it would most likely be a new variety, the "Improved Meyer lemon tree," developed by the University of California. The original Meyer lemon tree was found to be a carrier of citrus tristeza virus (CTV), so in 1975, all but one group of the original trees were destroyed and the new version released.

LEMON, PERRINE
Nº 112925
Citrus limon
Orlando, Orange County,
Florida, USA
L. C. C. Krieger, 1934

The Perrine variety is a cross between a West Indian lime
and a Genoa lemon. The name Perrine was given as a way
to pay homage to Dr Henry Perrine, a botanist and physician
who contributed greatly to the citrus industry during the
mid-1800s.

No. 40220
Green
Lemon

No. 40221
Ripe Lemon

Arlington Heights Fruit Co.
Riverside
Riverside Co. Cal.

E. I. Schutt
Jan 3- 07
Jan 11-'08

LEMON
Nº 40220 & 40221
Citrus limon
Riverside, Riverside County,
California, USA
E. I. Schutt, 1908

This illustration shows two specimens: No. 40220 is a green lemon and No. 40221 is a ripe lemon.

No. 50638.
"Mucor"
Green Cured 1 month
Stored 40°
C. W. Mann
Pasadena
Los Angeles Co., Calif.

E. I. Schutt
May 22d. 11.
Taken from moist
Chamber June 5 - '11.
June 6 - '11

Note:- Showing further development of dried brown area
around stem since fruit was put in moist chamber
May 22d with mucor and blue mold.

Picked Jan 10.

LEMON
Nº 50638a
Citrus limon
Pasadena, Los Angeles County,
California, USA
E. I. Schutt, 1911

Picked as a green fruit specimen on 10 January 1911, this
lemon was then cured for a month and stored at 40°F.
The fruit shows further development of the dry brown area
around the stem after it was put in a moist chamber on
22 May, and there is also evidence of mucor and blue mold.

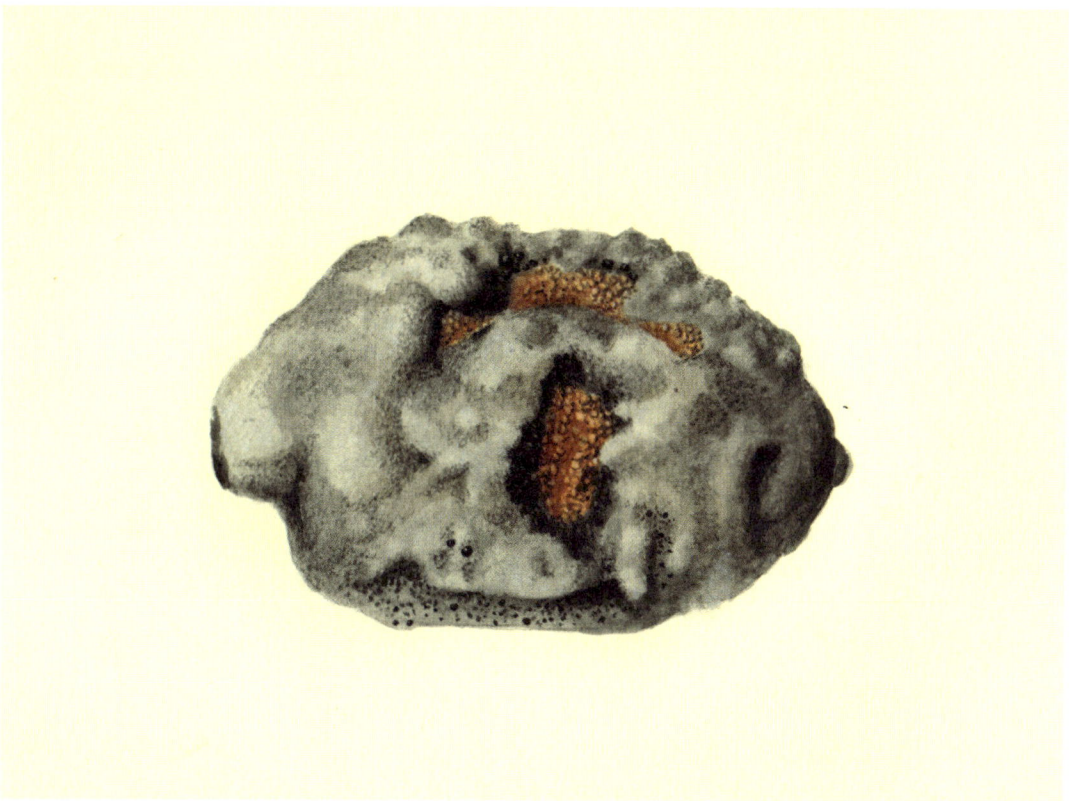

(top left) LEMON, Nº 264, *Citrus limon*, location unknown. J. M. Shull, 1909. Artificial inoculation. *(top right)* LIME, Nº 1135, *Citrus aurantiifolia*, location unknown. J. M. Shull, 1919. This specimen shows sour rot. *(bottom)* LEMON, Nº 317, *Citrus limon*, location unknown. J. M. Shull, 1910. Artificial inoculation by C. H. Hasse after 6 weeks.

86770
"Key"
L. B. Scott
Central Supply,
Fla.

Mary D. Arnold
12-4-15-
1-6-16

LIME, KEY
Nº 86770
Citrus aurantiifolia
Florida, USA
M. D. Arnold, 1916

This specimen was taken from the central supply by pomologist L. B. Scott. Key limes were commercially grown in the Florida Keys until a hurricane dramatically wiped out several groves in the 1920s. After the destruction, many farmers decided to replace the Key lime with the larger seedless Persian lime that is now more commonly sold in the US.

116

No 66990
Lisbon - Tree 1-26-16.
Sporting types in Spring bearing.
type of Lisbon tree
1 bottle shaped
1 protruding blossom end. L. B. Scott Corona Calif.

E. I. Schutt.
Nov. 6 - 13
Nov. 11 - 13.

LIME, LISBON
Nº 66990
Citrus aurantiifolia
Corona, Riverside County,
California, USA
E. I. Schutt, 1913

These fruits were taken from a spring-bearing type of citrus tree. The upper Lisbon lemon is bottle shaped and the lower lemon has been shaped by a protruding blossom end.

LIME
Nº 950
Citrus aurantiifolia
Corona, Riverside County,
California, USA
J. M. Shull, 1916

Lime culture in steamed rice. The tuber was inoculated on 8 September 1916. From left to right, strains No. 406, 901, and 504.

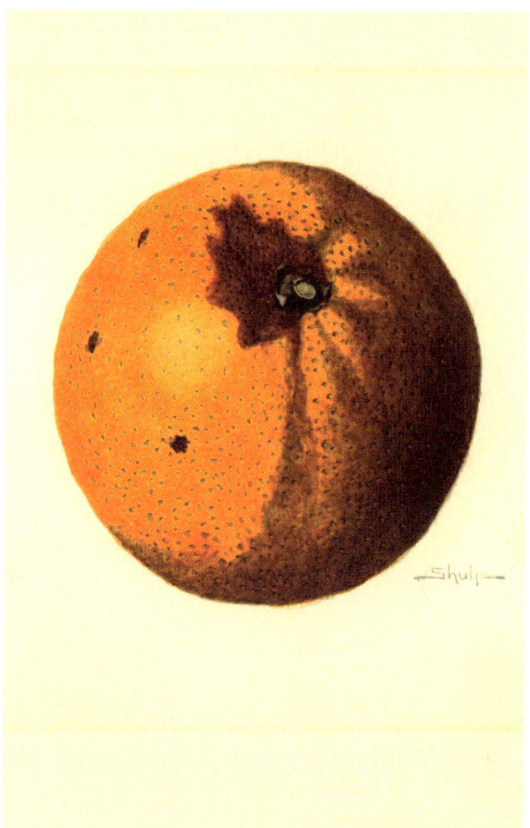

J. M. Shull studies of decay stages in oranges (*Citrus sinensis*).
(*top left*) Nº 1292a, location unknown, 1922. Experimentally produced. (*top right*) Nº 1528, Houma, Louisiana, USA, 1928. Sour orange. (*bottom left*) Nº 468, location unknown, 1912. Artificial inoculation. (*bottom right*) Nº 469, location unknown, n.d. Small artificial inoculations. Also, small infection at the stem end.

#17678
"Bishop's Favorite"
"World's Fair"
from A D Bishop, Orange, Orange Co
Cal.
D.G.Passmore

ORANGE, BISHOPS FAVORITE
Nº 17678
Citrus sinensis
Orange, Orange County,
California, USA
D. G. Passmore, circa 1899

120

ORANGE, FAIRAI SATSUMA
Nº 97222
Citrus sinensis
Foley, Baldwin County,
Alabama, USA
A. A. Newton, 1919

ORANGEQUAT, NIPPON
N° 112972
Citrus citrofortunella
Orlando, Orange County,
Florida, USA
M. D. Arnold, 1934

This specimen is a cross between a satsuma and a kumquat.

122

No. 95071

Mr. A. H. Leonard.
Winterhaven, Fla.

R. C. Steadman.
1-14-'18
1-9-'18

ORANGE
Nº 95071
Citrus sinensis
Winter Haven, Polk County,
Florida, USA
R. C. Steadman, 1918

ORANGE, WASHINGTON NAVEL
Nº 108998a
Citrus sinensis
Riverside, Riverside County,
California, USA
R. C. Steadman, 1927

124

ORANGE, WASHINGTON NAVEL
Nº 108998
Citrus sinensis
Riverside, Riverside County,
California, USA
R. C. Steadman, 1927

No 62659.
Yellow Navel Orange.
Type of Washington Nav'l.
A. B. Chamel. Riverside. Cal.
Grown at Sunny Mount. Ranch.
Tree 27/20. Picked 3/3/13.

E. J. Schutt
3 — 10 — '13
3 — 15 — '13

Tree 3/27/20

Showing characteristic stripe

ORANGE, WASHINGTON NAVEL
Nº 62659a
Citrus sinensis
Riverside, Riverside County,
California, USA
E. I. Schutt, 1913

126

The appearance of a "characteristic stripe," a segment of lighter or darker color on fruit skins is commonly referred to as a chimera, and is the result of a genetic mutation.

In Greek mythology the Chimera was a monstrous creature composed of the head of a lion, the body of a goat, and the tail of a snake. As a term in genetics, it describes a single organism made up of the cells from two or more genotypes (individual genetic organisms). A chimera in citrus fruits, in this case the Washington Navel orange, often results in a modification of the color of the fruit's rind, pulp, or shape.

The mutation can be explained by the fact that each section of a citrus fruit is nourished by specific leaves along the stem to which it is attached. The genetics of leaves feeding a fruit can therefore be different in neighboring sections, and this consequently results in the appearance of a "characteristic strip." Chimerism is a naturally occurring phenomenon and a potential source of new genetic material that can help improve a crop.

No. 43194,
"Dugats Improved"
Mrs. E. M. Dugat.
Beeville Bee Co. Texas

E. J. Schutt
Dec 31–'08
Feb. 6– '09

Duplicate made Dec 10–'09.

ORANGE, DUGATS IMPROVED
Nº 43194b
Citrus sinensis
Beeville, Bee County,
Texas, USA
E. I. Schutt, 1909

A duplicate of this illustration was produced on 10 December 1909.

ORANGE
Nº 69727
Citrus sinensis
Bahia, Nordeste, Brazil
M. D. Arnold, 1914

This illustration is annotated as a "standard type" of orange from this region in Brazil.

J. M. Shull studies of injured oranges (*Citrus sinensis*).
(top left) Nº 444, location unknown, 1911. *(top right)* Nº 1003, Orlando, Orange County, Florida, USA, 1917. *(bottom left)* Nº 1540, Plymouth, Orange County, Florida, USA, 1928. Cause of injury not known. Similar to spray injury, but the grove had not been sprayed. *(bottom right)* Nº 285, Florida, USA, 1910.

ORANGE
Nº 43654
Citrus sinensis
Florida, USA
A. A. Newton, 1909

A specimen of a diseased orange twig, noted to be caused by exanthema.

No. 96622
Dancy Tangerine.
R. L. Willits

R. C. Steadman.
1 – 7 – '19
12 – 30 – '18

TANGERINE, DANCY
N° 96622
Citrus reticulata
Location unknown
R. C. Steadman, 1919

No. 96605.
Francis Heiney.
Brawley Imperial Valley.
California.

R. C. Steadman.
12-21-'18
12-18-'18

TANGERINE, FRANCIS HEINEY
Nº 96605
Citrus reticulata
Brawley, Imperial County,
California, USA
R. C. Steadman, 1918

No. 98120.
Wase Satsuma.
Gosaku-Sueoka.
Ocho-maru, Toyoda-gun, Hiroshma, Japan.

R. C. Steadman.
1-7-'20.

SATSUMA, WASE SATSUMA
Nº 98120
Citrus unshiu
Hiroshima, Chugoku, Japan
R. C. Steadman, 1920

MANDARIN
Nº 103822
Citrus reticulata
Location unknown
R. C. Steadman, 1923

First discovered in the 18th century, the mandarin orange gets its name from the Swedish "mandarin apelsin"; "apelsin" comes from the German *Apfelsine*, which means "Chinese apple."

50309
King
C. S. Pomeroy
Tampa
Florida

Elsie E. Lower.
2 - 21 - 1911
3 - 4 - 1911

TANGOR, KING
Nº 50309
Citrus nobilis
Tampa, Hillsborough County,
Florida, USA
E. E. Lower, 1911

The tangor is a hybrid variety that is a cross between a mandarin orange (*Citrus reticulata*) and a sweet orange (*Citrus sinensis*).

408441/2
King
W. W. Irwin,
Mrs McCarthy,
1345 7 St. N.W.
D.C.

A. A. Newton
4-16-08
4-23-08

TANGOR, KING
Nº 40844 1/2a
Citrus nobilis
Washington, DC, USA
A. A. Newton, 1908

Drupes

D electable peaches, fragrant apricots, subtle plums, juicy nectarines, delightful cherries—there is something for every taste among the delightful drupes. There is, perhaps, a supplementary reason for stone fruits' widespread popularity: eating a drupe is a playful, slightly messy undertaking, which brings childish delight, and then, hands still sticky with sweet juice, comes the temptation to throw the kernel into a bush and the fleeting thought that a fruit tree might grow where it lands.

Investigating the origins of most stone fruit would lead us to ancient Asian civilizations, but peaches precede humankind. Fossilized peach kernels dating from the late Pliocene era were unearthed in Kunming, southwestern China—showing the fruit grew wild in the region more than two and a half million years ago. The peach has taken a central place in Chinese cuisine and culture across millennia. In mythology, the treasured Peaches of Immortality grew in the orchard of the Queen Mother of the West and were consumed by the *xian* (immortals).

The Peaches of Immortality were so precious that they were sometimes stolen. Such a crime was perpetrated by the *fangshi* (scholar) Dongfang Shuo, a former *xian* courtier of the Queen Mother of the West. As a punishment for his theft, he was temporarily banished to earth and his endlessness taken from him. The famous legend is illustrated in a 15th-century silk tapestry showing the scholar holding one of the cherished fruits beneath a lavish, blooming tree.

The cherry tree and its luscious fruit hold an equally emblematic and important place in folklore, as well as having many fascinating stories surrounding its diaspora. One such involves Ah Bing, a foreman in an orchard in Milwaukie, Oregon, where he had worked for 35 years. He was involved in, if not the actual originator of, a new cherry variety. Bing returned to his native China for a holiday, but was unable to return to North America because of the Chinese Exclusion Act of 1882. As a tribute to his work the fruit was named after him—today, the Bing cherry, distinguished by its dramatic dark color and firm flesh, is the most produced variety in the US.

Cherries originated in Japan, where *hanami,* the ritual of observing and honoring the *sakura* (cherry) blossom every spring has been practiced since the eighth century. In Japanese culture and art, cherry blossoms have come to symbolize the beauty and acceptance of the transience of life—epitomized in the concept of *mono no aware,* which can be translated as "sensitivity to ephemera." Kobayashi Issa, regarded as one of Japan's greatest poets, famously rendered the trees' emotive influence in the following haiku:

What a strange thing!
to be alive
beneath cherry blossoms.

The story of how cherry trees arrived in North America can be traced to Eliza Scidmore's admirable devotion and determination. She was an American author, geographer, and photographer, and the first woman to sit on the National Geographic

PLUM, YELLOW EGG
N° 00102
Prunus domestica
Location unknown
M. D. Arnold, 1939

Society's board of trustees. Over the course of her many trips to Japan, she fell in love with cherry trees and set about bringing them to her native land. In 1885 she first proposed her idea of planting a cherry forest in Washington, DC, which was met with little public interest—but Scidmore did not give up. It took her 24 years, but her plan finally came to fruition when First Lady Helen Taft, who herself had visited Japan and marveled at the trees, gave her support to the project. Helped by the USDA's David Fairchild and the Japanese consul, Scidmore organized the sending of 2,000 trees from Tokyo, which were given by Japan as gifts to the US in a gesture of diplomatic friendship. Unfortunately, the first cargo had to be burned due to worries about pest infestation. A second, healthy shipment of trees arrived in 1912 and became the famous *sakura* of West Potomac Park.

Carissa macrocarpa
Harpephyllum caffrum
Prunus angustifolia
Prunus avium
Prunus cerasifera var. *divaricata*
Prunus domestica
Prunus mume
Prunus persica
Prunus salicina
Prunus simonii
Prunus spinosa

142

No. 91150
"Mirabelle Tardive"
Geneva Exp. Sta.
Geneva, N.Y.

R. C. Steadman.
10-26-'16.
10-17-'16.

PLUM, MIRABELLE TARDIVE
Nº 91150
Prunus domestica
Geneva, Ontario County,
New York, USA
R. C. Steadman, 1916

48055
Mc Laughlin
R. A. Wellington
Exp Sta
Geneva - Ontario
N.Y.

D.G. Passmore
9.7.1910
9.8.1910

PLUM, MCLAUGHLIN
Nº 48055
Prunus domestica
Geneva, Ontario County,
New York, USA
D. G. Passmore, 1910

This specimen was taken from the New York State
Agricultural Experiment Station, Geneva.

Abundance Plum. Olcott Beach NY. 1903
belated + reduced in size from Little Peach.

PLUM, ABUNDANCE
№ 00083, 00086, 00087, 00088, 00089 & 00090
Prunus domestica
Olcott, Niagara County,
New York, USA
Artist unknown, 1903

A comparison illustration of healthy vs. diseased Abundance plums, showing how the fruit is belated in development and reduced in size and compared with the Little Peach variety.

#16110
Christian Steinman
Mapleton
Monona Co Iowa

D.G. Passmore
Tue Aug 17th 98

"Moldavka"

8-17-98

PLUM, MOLDAVKA
Nº 16110
Prunus domestica
Mapleton, Monona County,
Iowa, USA
D. G. Passmore, 1898

This specimen was taken from the South Haven Experiment
Station.

146

#13884
Kerr
from
J. H. Kerr,
Denton, Md.

B. Heiges
7/16/97

7 - 7 - 97

PLUM, KERR
Nº 13884
Prunus domestica
Denton, Caroline County,
Maryland, USA
B. Heiges, 1897

Studies of plums (*Prunus domestica*).
(*top left*) MADISON, Nº 6937, York, York County, Pennsylvania, USA. D. G. Passmore, 1894.
(*top right*) LANNIX, Nº 8839, Fayetteville, Cumberland County, North Carolina, USA.
D. G. Passmore, 1895. A letter written on the illustration on 7 November 1896 states this specimen
is a cross between a Bohan and a Wild Goose. (*bottom*) BURBANK, Nº 667, Chevy Chase,
Montgomery County, Maryland, USA. J. M. Shull, 1913. It is noted that 24 hours before the
blossoms normally open, some of the stamens were visibly filled at the bud stage. The buds are
also known to have experienced two successive mornings of 22°F temperature.

PLUM, SOPHIE
№ 3469
Prunus domestica
Denton, Caroline County,
Maryland, USA
D. G. Passmore, 1896

In China the plum blossom is one of the most beloved flowers and has for centuries been depicted in the country's art and poetry (see previous page, bottom image). There is a legend from ancient China that on the seventh day of the first lunar month, as the daughter of Emperor Wu of Liu Song rested under a plum tree, blossoms fell onto her face, leaving a floral imprint on her forehead that enhanced her beauty.

No. 95470.
"Pride of Florida"
A. Leyvraz.
Palatka, Fla.

R. G. Steadman.
5 — 11 - '18.
5 — 9 — '18

PLUM, PRIDE OF FLORIDA
Nº 95470
Prunus domestica
Palatka, Putnam County,
Florida, USA
R. C. Steadman, 1918

150

"Paisley"

#17673
Lauretta Paisley
from Mrs. Lauretta Paisley, Rob Roy, Fountain Co. Ind.
8/7/99

D.G. Passmore

PLUM, PAISLEY
Nº 17673
Prunus domestica
Rob Roy, Fountain County,
Indiana, USA
D. G. Passmore, 1899

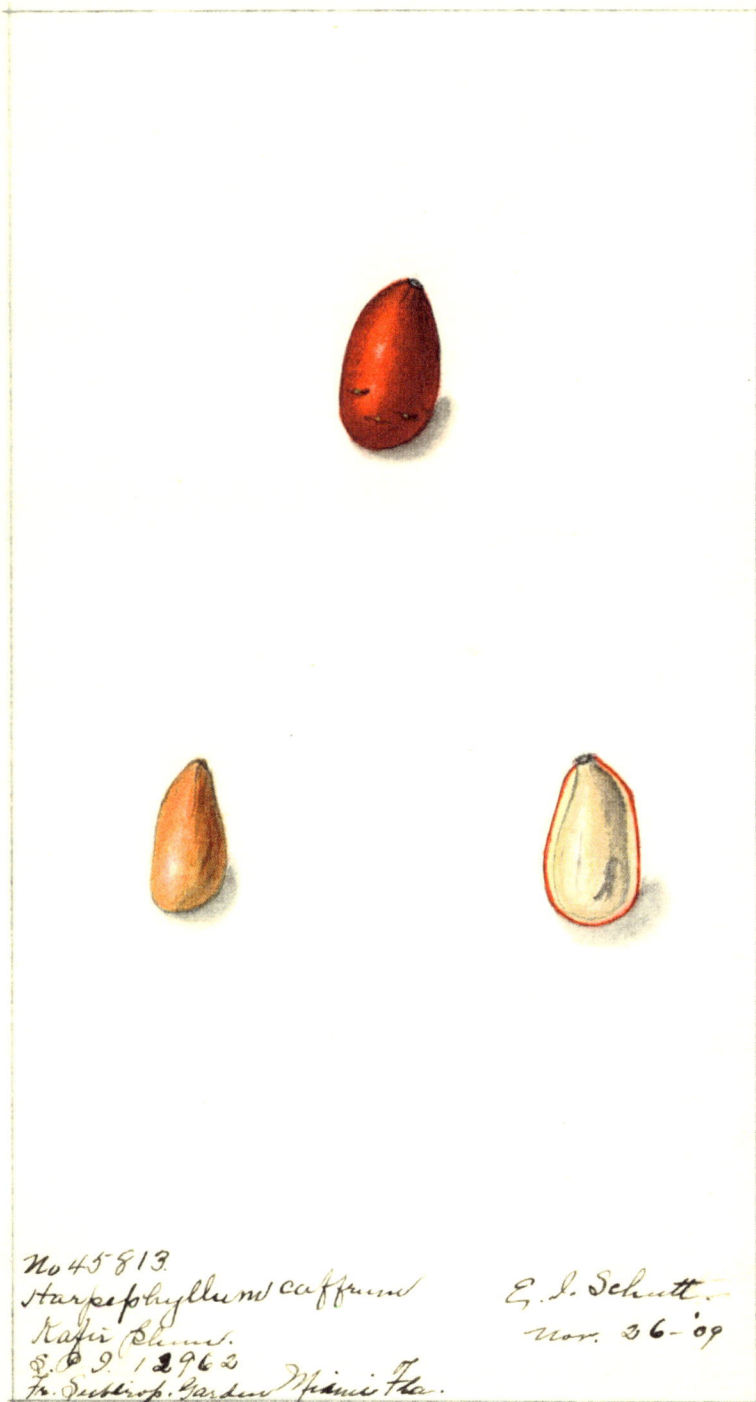

No 45813
Harpephyllum caffrum
Kafir Plum.
E P 9 12962
Fr. Subtrop. Garden Miami Fla.

E. I. Schutt.
nov. 26-'09

KAFFIR PLUM
Nº 45813
Harpephyllum caffrum
Miami, Dade County,
Florida, USA
E. I. Schutt, 1909

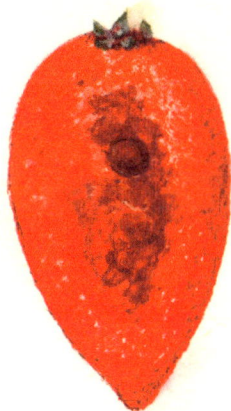

47082
Maritzgula
S. B. Bliss
Elkton Miami Co. Fla.
" Va.

D. G. Passmore
7. 5. 10
9. 15. 10

NATAL PLUM, MARITZGULA
Nº 47082
Carissa macrocarpa
Miami, Dade County,
Florida, USA
D. G. Passmore, 1910

PLUM, COLETTO
Nº x726 1/2   .
Prunus domestica
Nursery, Victoria,
Texas, USA
Artist unknown, 1888

Early Red
Prunus Chickasaw

From G. Onderdonk.

Nursery

Victoria Co. Texas

May 5th 1888

x677

CHICKASAW PLUM, EARLY RED
Nº x677
Prunus angustifolia
Nursery, Victoria,
Texas, USA
Artist unknown, 1888

Illinois Ironcla

PLUM, ILLINOIS IRONCLAD

N° 6969

Prunus domestica

Denton, Caroline County,
Maryland, USA

Artist unknown, n.d.

This variety is alternatively called American Eagle.

156

Prunus Simonii
#9035
J. A. Robinson
Snelling Merced Co
California
D. G. Passmore

APRICOT PLUM
Nº 9035
Prunus simonii
Snelling, Merced County,
California, USA
D. G. Passmore, 1895

21996
Delicious
Luther Burbank
Santa Rosa. Sonoma Co. Cal

D. G. Passmore.
8. 6. 1901

PLUM, DELICIOUS
Nº 21996
Prunus domestica
Santa Rosa, Sonoma County,
California, USA
D. G. Passmore, 1901

It is noted that the Flaming Delicious variety of plum, from
Stark's Burbank Collection, should be looked at in
conjunction with this illustration.

21900
Fraud
Luther Burbank, Santa Rosa, Sonoma Co. Calif.
D. G. Passmore
July 22 1901

PLUM, FRAUD
Nº 21900
Prunus domestica
Santa Rosa, Sonoma County,
California, USA
D. G. Passmore, 1901

PLUM, DAMSON
Nº 111528
Prunus domestica
Washington, DC, USA
R. C. Steadman, 1930

This variety was propagated for generations in Loudon Country, Virginia. Locally this plum was called an "old fashioned damson." This specimen was picked in the Takoma Park neighborhood of Washington, DC. The damson plum is well known for the length of time it takes to bear fruit, and there is even an ancient rhyme that goes, "He who plants plums, Plants for his sons. He who plants damsons, Plants for his grandsons."

PLUM, CRITTENDEN
Nº 111513
Prunus domestica
Washington, DC, USA
R. C. Steadman, 1930

This specimen was picked in the Takoma Park neighborhood of Washington, DC.

PLUM, TRAGEDY
Nº 113062
Prunus domestica
Penryn, Placer County,
California, USA
M. D. Arnold, 1935

PLUM, AGEN
Nº 105501
Prunus domestica
Sodus, Wayne County,
New York, USA
R. C. Steadman, 1924

(top) PLUM, Nº 366, *Prunus domestica*, Mount Rainier, Prince Georges County, Maryland, USA. J. M. Shull, 1910. The injured or diseased portions of the fruit are noted to be firm instead of soft as would be expected with brown rot. These specimens were sprayed with lime sulfur and lead arsenate. *(bottom left)* JAPANESE PLUM, Nº 00299, *Prunus salicina*, Washington, DC, USA. R. Cowing, 1890. *(bottom right)* JAPANESE PLUM, Nº 00314, *Prunus salicina*, Washington, DC, USA. The two bottom specimens were inoculated, and the section demonstrates visually the spread of the disease, in this case pear blight, and the larger air cavities that are produced by the fruit drying out.

20051

from
Prof. E. R. Lake
Carcassonne,
9/14/00   Dept. Aude, France.

B. Heiges
9/15/00

Coeur de Boeuf

PLUM, COEUR DE BOEUF
Nº 20051
Prunus domestica
Carcassonne,
Languedoc-Roussillon, France
B. Heiges, 1900

55

37

413

182

Wild sloe blackthorn fruits of the Caucasus.

BLACKTHORN
Nº 55, 37, 413 & 182
Prunus spinosa
Caucasus
Artist unknown, n.d.

166

CHERRY PLUM
Nº 00310
Prunus cerasifera var. *divaricata*
Caucasus
Artist unknown, n.d.

Wild cherry plums of the Caucasus.

Black Republican

3294

C. E. Hoskins.
Newberg.
Yamhill Co.

Wm. H. Prestele fecit

7 – 18 – 92

CHERRY, BLACK REPUBLICAN
Nº 3294
Prunus avium
Newberg, Yamhill County,
Oregon, USA
W. H. Prestele, 1892

CHERRY, MORREAU
Nº 113285
Prunus avium
Rosslyn, Arlington County,
Virginia, USA
R. C. Steadman, 1936

The color shown is from the dead-ripe condition of the fruit.

Marasca moscata cherry,
from arlington Farm,
July 10, 1933.
 # 112614

CHERRY, MARASCA MOSCATA
Nº 112614
Prunus avium
Rosslyn, Arlington County,
Virginia, USA
L. C. C. Krieger, 1933

170

No. 98375
Arlington 5049
Planted ao 33982
Arlington Farm.
Cherry - St. Medard.

R. C. Steadman.
6 - 19 - '20.

CHERRY, ST MEDARD
№ 98375
Prunus avium
Rosslyn, Arlington County,
Virginia, USA
R. C. Steadman, 1920

This specimen is noted to have been checked against others of its same crop and found to be entirely accurate in terms of its sizing, color, and other details.

CHERRY, LAMBERT
Nº 104974
Prunus avium
Toppenish, Yakima County,
Washington, USA
R. C. Steadman, 1924

172

CHERRY, OLIVET
No 82051
Prunus avium
Geneva, Ontario County,
New York, USA
A. A. Newton, 1915

This specimen was taken from the New York State
Agricultural Experiment Station, Geneva.

38457
Lambert
Miss Clara L. Webb
Troutville
Multnomah Co.
             Oregon.

D. G. Passmore
7.11.'07
7.16.07

CHERRY, LAMBERT
Nº 38457
Prunus avium
Troutdale, Multnomah County,
Oregon, USA
D. G. Passmore, 1907

The location name on the illustration, Troutville, was
corrected to Troutdale by the archive.

174

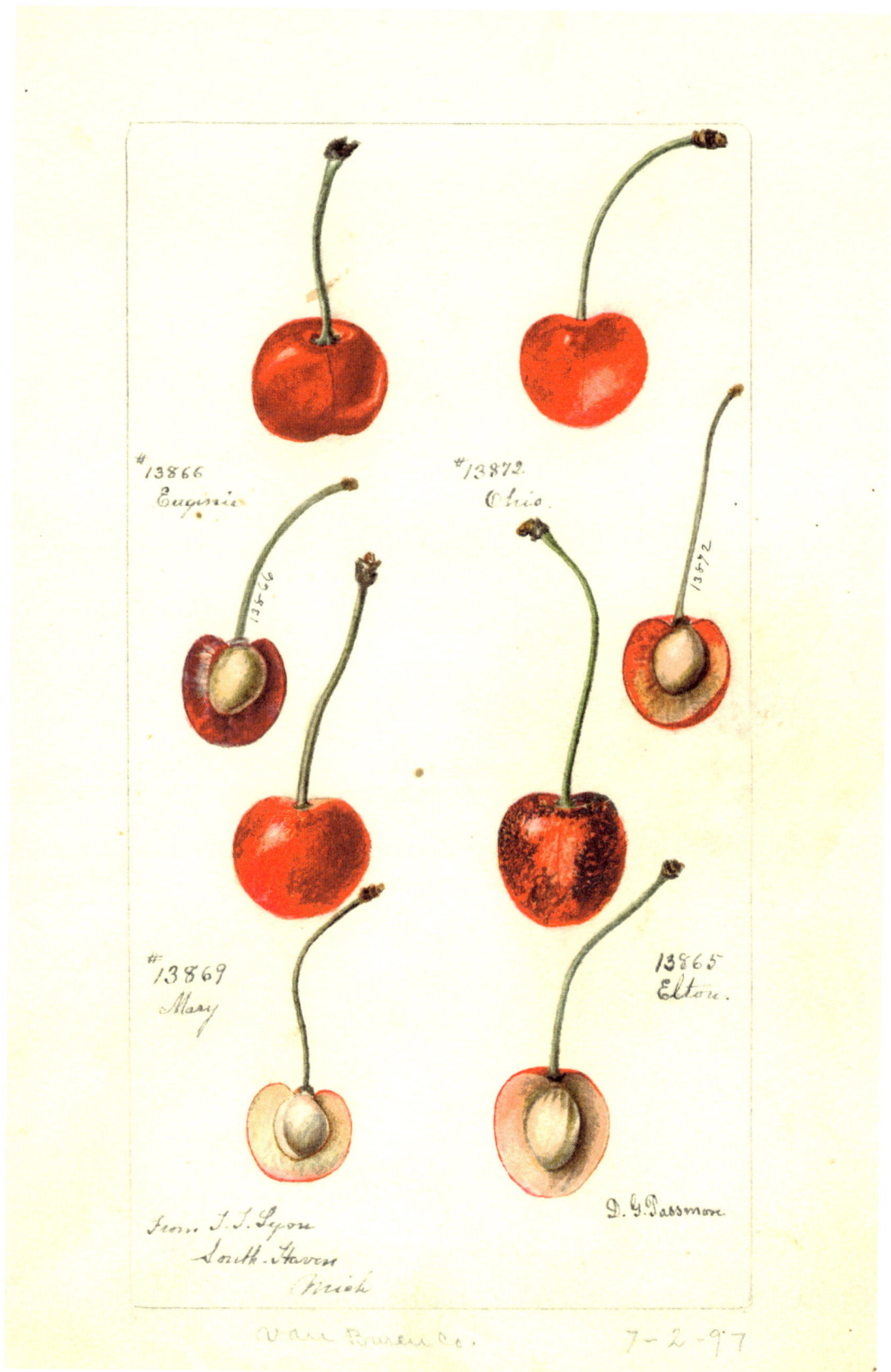

CHERRY
Nº 13866, 13872, 13869 & 13865
Prunus avium
South Haven, Van Buren County,
Michigan, USA
D. G. Passmore, 1897

This watercolor shows the varieties Eugenie, Ohio, Mary, and Elton.

Nv. 89117.
"Northwest."
Geneva Ex. Sta.
Geneva N.Y.

R. C. Steadman.
7-24-'16.
7-20-'16.

CHERRY, HORTENSE
Nº 89003
Prunus avium
Geneva, Ontario County,
New York, USA
R. C. Steadman, 1916

This specimen was taken from the New York State
Agricultural Experiment Station, Geneva.

176

CHERRY, BING
Nº 111000
Prunus avium
Washington, DC, USA
R. C. Steadman, 1929

This specimen was bought from a sanitation store as it was assumed to be the Bing variety.

#13863
Cleveland.

#13863
Cleveland.

#13873
Rockport (Big.)

#13873
Rockport.

#13863
#13873
from
T. T. Lyon
South Haven,
Mich.

B. Heiges
7/8/97

Van Buren Co.   7-2-97

CHERRY
Nº 13863 & 13873
Prunus avium
South Haven, Van Buren County,
Michigan, USA
B. Heiges, 1897

This watercolor shows the varieties Cleveland and Rockport.

178

CHERRY, WINDSOR
N° 47130
Prunus avium
Grimsby, Ontario, Canada
A. A. Newton, 1910

93367
"Buttner Yellow"
Stephen Harmeling,
Vashon, Washington

Mary D. Arnold
8-10-17

CHERRY, BUTTNERS YELLOW
№ 93367
Prunus avium
Vashon, King County,
Washington, USA
M. D. Arnold, 1917

7613
"Golden Beauty"
from S. S. Lyon
South Haven
Vanburen Co
Mich.

Rad 9/27/94

D. G. Passmore

9-27-94

CHERRY, GOLDEN BEAUTY
N° 7613
Prunus avium
South Haven, Van Buren County,
Michigan, USA
D. G. Passmore, 1894

(top) PEACH, Nº 1566, *Prunus persica*, Vienna, Fairfax County, Virginia, USA. J. M. Shull, 1931. This specimen shows the result of drought injury. The drought of 1931 that ruined so many crops, including peaches such as this example, began in 1930 and has since come to be characterized in American history as the Dust Bowl, or sometimes, colloquially, as the Dirty Thirties. *(bottom)* PEACH, HILEY, Nº 970, *Prunus persica*, Fort Valley, Peach County, Georgia, USA. J. M. Shull, 1917. This specimen shows the result of frost injury on the blossom of a peach tree. It is also noted that the illustration is scaled at twice the natural size of the blossom.

182

PEACH, EARLY RIVERS
Nº 306
Prunus persica
Woodwardville, Anne Arundel County,
Maryland, USA
J. M. Shull, 1910

This watercolor shows the branch and blossoms of a peach tree without the fruit.

Carman.
Exp. Station.
So. Haven, Mich.

R. G. Steadman.
8 – 20 – '19.

Arkansas.
Exp. Station.
So. Haven, Mich.

R. G. Steadman.
8 – 1 – '18

(top) PEACH, CARMAN № 8201919, *Prunus persica*, South Haven, Van Buren County, Michigan, USA. R. C. Steadman, 1919. *(bottom)* PEACH, ARKANSAS, № 811918, *Prunus persica*, South Haven, Van Buren County, Michigan, USA. R. C. Steadman, 1918. Both specimens were taken from the South Haven Agricultural Experiment Station.

Chinese Peach
Arnold Arboretum
Sept 7 - 93   Brookline —
Suffolk Co. Mass.
5355

D. G. Passmore

PEACH, CHINESE
Nº 5355
Prunus persica
Brookline, Norfolk County,
Massachusetts, USA
D. G. Passmore, 1893

No 42027.
Seedling "Keith".
Dr. A. B. Dennis
Mr. B. Keith
Cedar Rapids
Linn Co., Iowa.

E. I. Schutt
Sept 15 "08
16 - "08.

PEACH, KEITH
№ 42027
Prunus persica
Cedar Rapids, Linn County,
Iowa, USA
E. I. Schutt, 1908

This specimen is noted to be a seedling. The peach was one of the first fruits to have been eaten on the moon, during the Apollo 11 mission.

44478. 44479
Early Crawford
M. B. Waite,
Mr. Smith,
Grimsby
Ont.
9-17-'09. 9-20-'09
A. A. Newton.

PEACH
Nº 44478 & 44479
Prunus persica
Grimsby, Ontario, Canada
A. A. Newton, 1909

This watercolor shows the varieties Early Crawford and Little Peach.

44027
Wild Peach.
J. Fulkerson.
Fallon
Churchill Co.
Nev.

Elsie E. Lower.
8-6-'09
8-10-'09

PEACH, WILD
Nº 44027
Prunus persica
Fallon, Churchill County,
Nevada, USA
E. E. Lower, 1909

51261

"Hileys"
S. H. Fulton
Sleepy Creek,
Morgan Co.
W. Va.

M. Arnold.
8-15-11
8-25-11

PEACH, HILEY
Nº 51261
Prunus persica
Sleepy Creek, Morgan County,
West Virginia, USA
M. D. Arnold, 1911

NECTARINE, QUETTA
Nº 1645
Prunus persica
Location unknown
J. M. Shull, 1935

NECTARINE, QUETTA
Nº 1701
Prunus persica
Beltsville, Prince Georges County,
Maryland, USA
J. M. Shull, 1936

No. 95487
Persica - nectarina
From Exp. Station
Troup, Texas.

R. C. Steadman.
8 - 19 - '18
6 - 14 - '18

NECTARINE, PERSICA
Nº 95487
Prunus persica
Troup, Smith County,
Texas, USA
R. C. Steadman, 1914

This specimen was taken from the Texas Agricultural
Experiment Station.

NECTARINE
Nº 43143
Prunus persica
Location unknown
A. A. Newton, 1921

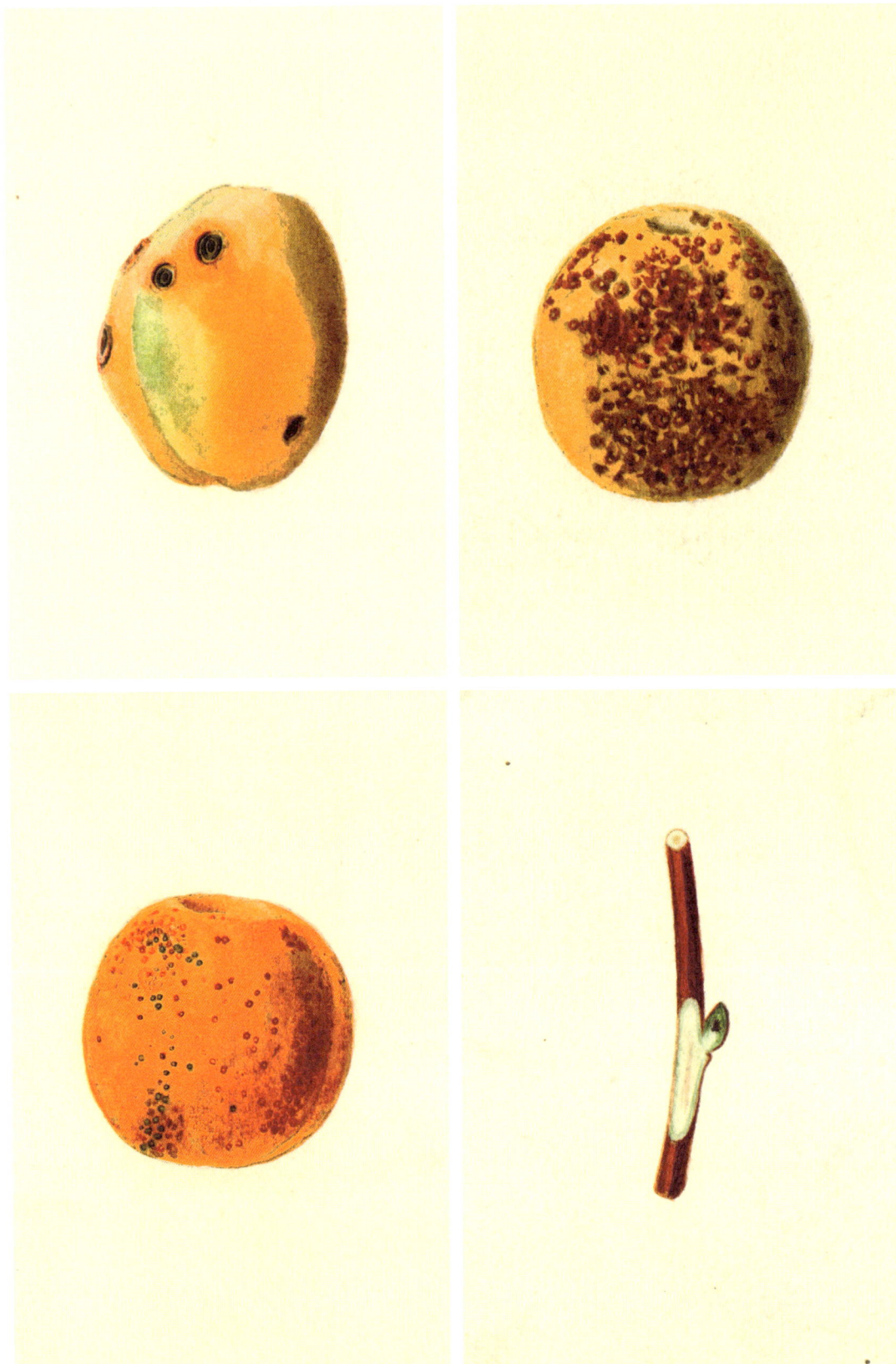

Studies by J. M. Shull of Japanese apricots (*Prunus mume*).
(top left) Nº 809, Wenatchee, Chelan County, Washington, USA, 1914. This specimen shows the result of scab on the fruit; however, it is also noted that the soil conditions could have caused similar damage. *(top right)* Nº 808, Eckert, Orchard City, Delta County, Colorado, USA, 1914. This specimen and the following also show the result of scab on the fruit. *(bottom left)* Nº 800, Idaho, USA, 1914. *(bottom right)* Nº 1389, Bitterroot, Montana, USA, 1925. This specimen shows the result of frost injury on the wood of the apricot plant.

JAPANESE APRICOT, VARIETY 9834
Nº 46905
Prunus mume
San Saba, San Saba County,
Texas, USA
A. A. Newton, 1910

The Japanese apricot is alternatively called the Chinese plum.

"Sharpe"
81972
M. Sharpe,
Vacaville,
Calif.

A. A. Newton.
7 - 1915
7-2-1915

JAPANESE APRICOT, SHARPE
Nº 81972a
Prunus mume
Vacaville, Solano County,
California, USA
A. A. Newton, 1915

196

JAPANESE APRICOT, BENNET
N° 93364
Prunus mume
Oden, Weber County,
Utah, USA
A. A. Newton, 1917

JAPANESE APRICOT
Nº 109123
Prunus mume
Chico, Butte County,
California, USA
R. C. Steadman, 1927

198

JAPANESE APRICOT
Nº 109124
Prunus mume
Chico, Butte County,
California, USA
R. C. Steadman, 1927

Berries & Small Fruit

34154
"Dornan"
F. A. Farrand,
South Haven
Van Buren Co., Mich.
6/16/05

B. Heiges
6/17/05

S weet, vibrant, juicy, luxurious, colorful and opulent—the attractive qualities of berries and grapes are plentiful, giving them the status, worldwide, of both beloved kitchen staples and symbols in numerous mythical traditions and folktales.

Native to Western Asia and the Caucasus, wild grapes were most likely the first food humans used to both nourish and inebriate themselves. As early as 7000 BCE, the ancient Chinese were drinking a fermented beverage made from grapes. Over the millennia, winemaking closely followed the fruit's odyssey to the Middle East and Europe. Grapes, symbolically inseparable from wine, came to represent indulgence, abundance, pleasure, and lust in art and literature. Dionysus, the Greek the god of the grape harvest, is frequently represented with a drinking cup and fruiting grapevines, as in Caravaggio's *Bacchus** (1596), in a deeply sensual scene where the young god seems to invite the viewer to succumb to hedonism. In the myth of the creation of wine, Dionysus falls in love with a handsome satyr named Ampelos. Carefree in character, Ampelos decides to ride a wild bull, is gored, and dies. Grief-stricken, Dionysus transforms the body of his beloved into the first grapevine and makes wine of his blood.

Berries also have a long-held place in folklore. The Virginia strawberry appears in a Cherokee tale surrounding the first married man and woman. After the couple argue for the first time, the woman walks away. To find his wife and apologize, the man seeks help from the sun, who then grows different kinds of berries on the woman's path in the hope that she will stop. She is unmoved by the plants until she encounters one with shiny green leaves, aromatic white flowers, and lush red berries, which pleases her. As she eats the strawberry, her anger fades and she goes home to reconcile with her husband. To this day, strawberries abound in the Southeastern Woodlands of the United States and are kept in Cherokee homes as a symbol of good fortune and as a reminder to make peace with loved ones.

Yet the idol of American berries remains the modest scarlet cranberry. Indigenous peoples consumed them dried to survive the frosty winter months, but today they are mostly taken as juice, jam, and, most significantly, the classic sauce to accompany traditional Thanksgiving turkey. The sauce is so crucial to that festive feast that when, in 1944, the US faced a cranberry shortage (caused by the weather, not the war), the USDA's *Homemakers' Chat* broadcast came to the distressed nation's rescue, providing suggestions and recipes for cranberry substitutes—and thus that year, in lieu of the long-established, glowing holiday sauce, Thanksgiving tables groaned with spiced peaches, syrupy pears, orange and raw carrot salad in gelatin, and watermelon pickles.

It would be remiss to write of small fruit without a mention of the actual picking of wild berries—an intrinsically sweet adventure that sharpens the senses and seldom fails to spark nostalgia. In his 1915 poem "Blueberries," Robert Frost celebrates

*Bacchus is Dionysus's Roman equivalent.

STRAWBERRY, DORNAN
N° 34154
Fragaria
South Haven, Van Buren County,
Michigan, USA
B. Heiges, 1905

203

blueberry picking—the smell of the morning dew, the feeling of the first rays of sunshine, and the delight in being the first to discover a ripe patch of fruit:

You ought to have seen
what I saw on my way
To the village, through
Mortenson's pasture to-day:
Blueberries as big as
the end of your thumb,
Real sky-blue, and heavy,
and ready to drum
In the cavernous pail
of the first one to come!
And all ripe together,
not some of them green
And some of them ripe!
You ought to have seen!

Fragaria
Morus
Ribes
Rubus
Rubus chamaemorus
Rubus idaeus
Rubus neglectus
Rubus occidentalis
Rubus phoenicolasius
Rubus subg. *Rubus* Watson
Vaccinium corymbosum
Vaccinium macrocarpon
Vitis

BLUEBERRY, STANLEY
Nº 1863
Vaccinium corymbosum
Location unknown
J. M. Shull, 1940

The Stanley blueberry, famed for its delicious taste, is a cross between the Katharine blueberry and the wild Rubel bush.

(top) BLUEBERRY, CATAWBA, Nº 1857, *Vaccinium corymbosum,* location unknown. J. M. Shull, 1940. *(bottom)* BLUEBERRY, REDSKIN, Nº 1856, *Vaccinium corymbosum,* location unknown. J. M. Shull, 1940. Both the top and bottom specimens are hybrids, of *Vaccinium corymbosum* L. and *Vaccinium angustifolium* Aiton.

BLUEBERRY, BROOKS
Nº 1860
Vaccinium corymbosum
Whitesbog, Burlington County,
New Jersey, USA
J. M. Shull, 1940

This specimen is noted to have been collected in the wild.
In the 1600s, American colonists found that if they boiled
blueberries with milk, they could produce a grey paint. Today
the blueberry fruit is the official berry of Nova Scotia, and
since 2004 the highbush species has been the official state
fruit of New Jersey.

65264
Jumbo
H. B. Scammel
Pemberton.
N. J.

Mary D. Arnold
9 - 26 - 13
5 - 16 - 14

AMERICAN CRANBERRY, JUMBO
Nº 65264
Vaccinium macrocarpon
Pemberton, Burlington County,
New Jersey, USA
M. D. Arnold, 1914

The cranberry plant is native to North America, and today Wisconsin is the top producer of the fruit in the US. The small fruit was originally named "cranberry" because it was thought that the plant's nodding elongated bloom resembles the head of a crane.

65260
Early Black
H. B Scammel
Pemberton,
N. J.

Mary D. Arnold
9-26-13
5-15-14

AMERICAN CRANBERRY, EARLY BLACK
№ 65260
Vaccinium macrocarpon
Pemberton, Burlington County,
New Jersey, USA
M. D. Arnold, 1914

In 1667 ten barrels of American cranberries were sent by New Englanders as a gift to appease King Charles II. In 1816, Captain Henry Hall became the first person to commercially grow cranberries in East Dennis, Massachusetts, on Cape Cod, which to this day remains one of the largest cranberry producers in America.

GOOSEBERRY, MOUNTAIN
Nº x18008
Ribes
Pewaukee, Waukesha County,
Wisconsin, USA
F. Muller, 1891

The gooseberry fruit has a sweet tangy taste that some
equate to being a mixture of a pineapple and a strawberry.
The fruit is native to England, and its commonness there
made it a staple in cooking during the country's colonial
days; however, many of these recipes have now disappeared
from cookbooks.

GOOSEBERRY
Nº 19594 & 19620
Ribes
Highland County,
Ohio, USA
D. G. Passmore & B. Heiges, 1900

This watercolor shows the following varieties: No. 19594, wild—*Ribus cynosbatis*, Henry W. Hope, Paint, Highland County, Ohio; No. 19620, mountain, Will S. Stover, Hope, Bartholomew County, Indiana. The artwork label states the location as Highland County, Ohio, in the archive.

13854
"White Smith"
from
Peder Pederson,
Huntingdon Valley,
Penn'a.

B. Heiges,
7/10/97

Montgomery Co.   7-1-97

GOOSEBERRY, WHITE SMITH
Nº 13854
Ribes
Huntingdon Valley, Montgomery
County, Pennsylvania, USA
B. Heiges, 1897

"Industry"
#15857
Katherine Chase
"Edgewood"
Washington. D.C.
D. G. Passmore
misc.
7-2-98

GOOSEBERRY, INDUSTRY
№ 15857
Ribes
Washington, DC, USA
D. G. Passmore, 1899

This specimen was picked in the Edgewood neighborhood of Washington, DC.

564334

Millionaire

Klondyke

STRAWBERRY
Nº 564334
Fragaria
Location unknown
M. D. Arnold, 1912

This watercolor shows leaves and blossoms of the varieties Millionaire and Klondyke.

STRAWBERRY, TENNESSEE
Nº 28702-1, 28702a & 28702b
Fragaria
West End, Fairfax County,
Virginia, USA
D. G. Passmore, n.d.

This illustration shows the result of cold storage on specimen No. 28702a. There is evidence of discoloration in bruised areas five days after storing in specimen No. 28702b, and the appearance of black mold in specimen No. 28702c five days after delayed storage.

#13778
"Dew" from G. M. Donaldson +6
Georgetown +6
I.G. Passmore
6-9-97

STRAWBERRY, DEW
Nº 13778
Fragaria
Washington, D. C, USA
D. G. Passmore, 1897

This specimen is noted to have been received from Georgetown in Washington, DC. The scientific name for strawberry, *Fragaria*, is derived from the Latin *fragare*, meaning "to be fragrant." The only fruit bearing seeds on the outside of the skin, each berry has an average of 200. Madame Tallien, the Spanish-born French noble and a prominent figure in the courts of Emperor Napoleon, became famous for bathing in the fresh juice of this sweet fruit.

(all) These specimens are a cross between the Chesapeake and Fairfax strawberry varieties.
(top) STRAWBERRY, STARBRIGHT, Nº 00079, *Fragaria*, location unknown. Artist unknown, n.d.
(bottom) STRAWBERRY, STARBRIGHT, Nº 00080. *Fragaria*, location unknown. Artist unknown, n.d.

STRAWBERRY, TIMBRELL
Nº 13761
Fragaria
Washington, DC, USA
D. G. Passmore, 1897

STRAWBERRY, GOLDEN GATE
N° 46849
Fragaria
College Park, Prince Georges County,
Maryland, USA
E. E. Lower, 1910

No. 38714
"Chamaemorus"
Allan MacLeod
Ferguson Lake
Richmond Co.
Cape Breton, Nova Scotia
Chamaemorus

E. I. Schutt
Aug 22 – 1907.

CLOUDBERRY
Nº 38714
Rubus chamaemorus
Ferguson Lake, Cape Breton Island,
Nova Scotia, Canada
E. I. Schutt, 1907

In both Finland and Norway there are strict rules concerning the picking of cloudberries, and Sweden has a department devoted to cloudberry disputes within its Ministry of Foreign Affairs.

WINEBERRY
№ 6769
Rubus phoenicolasius
York, York County,
Pennsylvania, USA
W. H. Prestele, 1894

Famous in both Japan and Korea, the wineberry, or *Rubus phoenicolasius*, is a species of raspberry that is indigenous to northern China.

81811
"Brinkles
  Orange"
Dr. Shoemaker
Horticulture

Mary T. Arnold
6-15-15

RED RASPBERRY, BRINKLES ORANGE
Nº 81811
Rubus idaeus
Location unknown
M. D. Arnold, 1915

RED RASPBERRY, MILLER
Nº 8886
Rubus idaeus
Seaford, Sussex County,
Delaware, USA
D. G. Passmore, 1895

According to Greek myth, raspberries were originally white and became red when the nymph Ida pricked her finger on the berry, staining the fruit forever the color of her blood. In Latin, *rubus* means "red" and *idaeus* means "belonging to Ida."

31675
Cuthbert.
J. K. Brown,
Lincolnia,
6/30/04 Fairfax Co., Va.

B. Heiges
7/11/04

RED RASPBERRY, CUTHBERT
Nº 31675
Rubus idaeus
Lincolnia, Fairfax County,
Virginia, USA
B. Heiges, 1904

RASPBERRY, MILLER & KANSAS
Nº 35653 & 35709
Rubus
Location unknown
Artist unknown, n.d.

This specimen was double wrapped and subject to eight months of 12°F cold storage, at the Central Market Cold Storage facilities in Washington, DC.

(top) PURPLE RASPBERRY, HAYMAKER, № 00288, *Rubus neglectus*, South Haven, Van Buren County, Michigan, USA. R. C. Steadman, 1918. This specimen was taken from the South Haven Agricultural Experiment Station. *(bottom)* BLACK RASPBERRY, HOPKINS & OHIO, № x15060 & x15059, *Rubus occidentalis*, Maysville, Mason County, Kentucky, USA. Artist unknown, 1891. It is noted that the varieties shown have been transposed, and the black raspberry to the left is actually a Hopkins.

PURPLE RASPBERRY, SHAFFER
Nº x14030 1/2
Rubius neglectus
Four Mile Run,
Virginia, USA
Artist unknown, 1891

The purple raspberry was first developed by the New York State Agricultural Experiment Station, Geneva. The fruit is a horticultural hybridization of red and black raspberries, and can be found growing wild in places like Vermont. Although you might be able to find the berries in local farmers' markets, the commercial production of this variety is rare due to the fruit being too soft for shipping.

40862
Travis
E. W. Kirkpatrick
McKinney – Collin Co. Tex.

D. G. Passmore
5 . 2 . 1908
5 . 7 . 1908

MULBERRY, TRAVIS
Nº 40862
Morus

McKinney, Collin County,
Texas, USA
D. G. Passmore, 1908

Morus, the Latin term for mulberries, is a fruit tree native to China, where
it was traditionally cultivated for its leaves and berries as a food source
for silkworms. The trees were adopted in Europe with the expansion of
the Silk Road, and in early colonial times were introduced into America.
The fruit is associated with evil spirits in Germany. In ancient Greece the
mulberry was dedicated to Minerva, the goddess of wisdom.

228

MULBERRY, COLOWAY
Nº 40861
Morus
McKinney, Collin County,
Texas, USA
E. E. Lower, 1908

Vincent van Gogh famously featured mulberry trees in some of his paintings, capturing what he describes as their "bushy foliage" and "magnificent yellow against a very blue sky."

Johnston's Sweet

APPROVED:
CHIEF C. DIV.
ILLUSTRATIONS.

BLACK RASPBERRY, JOHNSTONS SWEET
N° x16076
Rubus occidentalis
New York, USA
F. Muller, 1891

The illustrations featured above and on the following page show a stamp of approval from the Chief of the Division of Illustrations.

F. Muller.

Doolittle #x15080
Maurice Leonard
Oakland Mills Pa
July 7th 1891

APPROVED:
CHIEF OF DIV.
ILLUSTRATIONS.

BLACK RASPBERRY, DOOLITTLE
Nº x15080
Rubus occidentalis
Oakland Mills, Juniata County,
Pennsylvania, USA
F. Muller, 1891

Rubus occidentalis, commonly named the black raspberry, is also occasionally referred to as "black-caps," a term it shares with wild blackberries that grow in various parts of the United States.

BLACKBERRY, MERSEREAU
Nº 101557
Rubus subg. *Rubus* Watson
Location unknown
R. C. Steadman, 1922

No. 89086.
"Ohmer."
Md. Agr. Exp. Sta.
College Park. Md.

R. C. Steadman.
7-25-'16.
7-18-'16.

BLACKBERRY, OHMER
N° 89086
Rubus subg. *Rubus* Watson
College Park, Prince Georges County,
Maryland, USA
R. C. Steadman, 1916

21924
"Iceberg"
Meyer + Son,
Bridgeville, Sussex Co., Del.
7/23/01

B. Heiges
7/24/01

BLACKBERRY, ICEBERG
N° 21924
Rubus subg. *Rubus* Watson
Bridgeville, Sussex County,
Delaware, USA
B. Heiges, 1901

The Iceberg variety of blackberry is an unusual white variety of the fruit that was developed by the plant breeder Luther Burbank. Burbank was a botanist who over his 55-year career establish some 800 other strains and varieties of plants in the US. He only successfully created this variety in 1894 after some 65,000 failed crossbreeding attempts at his facility in Santa Rosa, California.

Americus (Seedling No 1) ?
Blackberry # 14017
L.H. Langille
Kensington
Montgomery co md   7-27-97

BLACKBERRY, AMERICUS
N° 14017
Rubus subg. *Rubus* Watson
Kensington, Montgomery County,
Maryland, USA
Artist unknown, 1897

This specimen is noted as Americus Seedling No. 1.

BRAMBLE, ROWAND
Nº 22928a
Rubus
Eckington,
Washington, DC, USA
D. G. Passmore, 1901

In British folklore, when St Michael cast the devil out of
heaven, he fell and landed on a bramble bush, and cursed
it in the process. The berries are thought to be unpalatable
from 29 September (St Michael's Day)—the last day to pick
them. The bramble's reputation has shifted as of late, and
is considered a useful tool in forensic botany due to their
distinctive growth pattern.

BRAMBLE
Nº 104995
Rubus
Beltsville, Prince Georges County,
Maryland, USA
R. C. Steadman, 1924

38348
White Staminat.
E. F. Cole
Fayetteville
Cumberland Co
N. C.

D. G. Passmore
5. 17. 07

GRAPE, WHITE STAMINATE
Nº 38348
Vitis
Fayetteville, Cumberland County,
North Carolina, USA
D. G. Passmore, 1907

This specimen has staminate flowers.

Flowers Grape

James Grape

Flowers and James Grapes.

GRAPE, JAMES & FLOWERS
Nº 00188 & 00189
Vitis
Napa, Napa County,
California, USA
A. A. Newton, n.d.

This watercolor is a mockup for the *Yearbook of Agriculture 1913*. It is noted that the varieties shown are Flowers and James.

GRAPE, MEMORY
№ 36740
Vitis
Whiteville, Columbus County,
North Carolina, USA
E. E. Lower, 1906

GRAPE, CONCORD
Nº 26361
Vitis
Washington, DC, USA
D. G. Passmore, 1902

This specimen is noted as an example of a "double grape." Named after the Massachusetts village of Concord, this variety was first encountered in 1849 when Boston-born Ephraim Wales Bull developed it there in 1849. The Concord today is known for its multiple uses that range from jellies to wines, giving the fruit a substantial place in the food market.

241

GRAPE, FREDONIA
Nº 00190
Vitis
Location unknown
R. C. Steadman, n.d.

The Fredonia variety of grape has a large crop with a blue-black color. It ripens around two weeks before the Concord.

(top left) GRAPE, PRESIDENT, Nº 00221, *Vitis,* location unknown. R. C. Steadman, n.d.
(top right) GRAPE, MANITO, N. 00205, *Vitis,* location unknown. R. C. Steadman, n.d.
(bottom left) GRAPE, NECTAR, Nº 00210, *Vitis,* location unknown. Artist unknown, n.d.
(bottom left) GRAPE, ALEXANDER WINTER, Nº 00157, *Vitis,* location unknown. J. M. Shull, n.d.

51577
Muscat Noir ded Hangrie
Fred Husmann,
Fresno, Calif.

A.A.Newton.

GRAPE, MUSCAT NOIR DE HANGRIE
Nº 51577
Vitis
Fresno, Fresno County,
California, USA
A. A. Newton, n.d.

GRAPE, ROSE D'ITALIE
Nº 49005
Vitis
Napa, Napa County,
California, USA
E. E. Lower, 1910

It is noted that Mr Arnold would be sending a cutting of this specimen back to George C. Husmann (expert in charge of viticultural investigations at the Bureau of Plan Industry, USDA) after it was discovered they had gotten the sample mixed.

GRAPE, REQUA
Nº 00225
Vitis
Location unknown
R. C. Steadman, n.d.

At the time these illustrations were authored, grape production in the USA was on the rise. The USDA's *Yearbook of Agriculture 1925* includes an account of "100 per cent increase in the acreage of vines and grapes produced and in [the] various uses made of grapes," between 1899 and 1909. Grape uses at this time in America included wine, raisins, canned, dried, and unfermented juice. Wine production is a lucrative and widespread reason for growing grapes in the US today, with all 50 states now having commercial wine industries. The rate of consumption of domestically produced wine outweighs that of imported wine two to one.

Also coinciding with the creation of these illustrations, grape production suffered large problems because of black rot and the endemic disease of mildew, which, as is stated in *A History of Wine in America* by Thomas Pinney, "put every grower's crop at risk season after season."

The varieties of grapes produced in America's reddish, sandy loam and porous soil in the early 20th century were at a promising point of adaptability, development, and hybridization. But this process was disrupted by prohibition laws introduced in 1920, which arrested the demand for grapes to be used in wine-making for the following 13 years.

42209
F. L. Husmann,
Fresno,
Fresno Co.
Calif.

"Panariti"
PANARITI

GRAPE, PANARITI
№ 42209
Vitis
Fresno, Fresno County,
California, USA
A. A. Newton, 1908

No. 53889
Rodites
F. L. Husmann
Oakville Exp. Vin.
California.

E. I. Schutt.
Dec. 4 – '11

GRAPE, RODITES
Nº 53889
Vitis
California, USA
E. I. Schutt, 1911

This specimen came from F. L. Husmann at the Oakville Experiment Vineyard.

#20090
Dracut Amber
W. N. Irwin
Eckington. D.C.

D. G. Passmore
9.20.1900

GRAPE, DRACUT AMBER
№ 20090
Vitis
Washington, DC, USA
D. G. Passmore, 1900

This specimen was picked in the Eckington neighborhood of Washington, DC.

GRAPE, SCUPPERNONG
Nº 38369
Vitis
Fayetteville, Cumberland County,
North Carolina, USA
A. A. Newton, 1907

As the state fruit of North Carolina, the Scuppernong grape was suitably named after North Carolina's Scuppernong River. It is a variety of grape that is a variant of the muscadine and bear the scientific name *Vitis rotundifolia*, meaning "vine with a round leaf."

GRAPE, DUTCHESS
Nº 00181
Vitis
Location unknown
R. C. Steadman, n.d.

The Dutchess grape was introduced to America in the 1890s, and was consequently named after the Dutchess County in New York. A pale green and crisp berry, it is typically used to make sweet and fruity wine.

GRAPE, ONTARIO
Nº 00244
Vitis
Location unknown
M. D. Arnold, 1933

GRAPE, HYCALES
Nº 45110
Vitis
Napa, Napa County,
California, USA
E. I. Schutt, 1909

41482
Lady Washington
Jas. H. Ricketts
638 G. St. S.E.
Washington D.C.

D.G. Passmore
8.14.08
8.20.08

GRAPE, LADY WASHINGTON
Nº 41482
Vitis
Washington, DC, USA
D. G. Passmore, 1908

Melons

257

J. Passmore
15. 1. 98

Thirst-quenching, succulent, invigorating, salubrious—melons sweeten long and lazy scorching summer days. But a certain mystery, as well as a seeming capriciousness, surrounds this most palatable of fruits. Melons can only be eaten in the brief period when they achieve perfect ripeness; unlike most fruits, their sugar content starts to decrease on being separated from the vine. The French poet Claude Mermet alluded to this volatility in 1600, at a time when melons were particularly fashionable in Europe:

> Friends are like Melons.
> Shall I tell you why?
> To find one good,
> you must a hundred try.

Finding a melon in which sweetness and firmness coexist harmoniously is no easy undertaking, whatever the favored technique of appraisal: smelling, analyzing the sound a candidate gives on being knocked gently, weighing, or pressing both ends. And melons are large enough for several servings—they are seemingly meant to be enjoyed in company—so should you pick a fruit not as splendid as it might be, group disappointment will surely follow.

Melons are part of the Cucurbitaceae family, which also encompasses cucumbers, squash, and an array of other gourds. Endowed with flamboyant scarlet flesh and a distinctive striped green skin, the grand watermelon imposes itself as one of the most delectable varieties, from both aesthetic and gustatory points of view. Originating in Africa, the watermelon was cultivated in ancient Egypt over 4,000 years ago— watermelon seeds have been discovered in the tomb of Tutankhamun. The reason the fruit was prized in that arid country lies in its name: its high water content means it can store water during the dry months and be taken on long expeditions as it remains edible for weeks—even months—if kept in the shade. Watermelons were grown widely in the Southern states during the Civil War, and inspired several American artists and authors, including Mark Twain, who wrote in his 1894 novel *Pudd'nhead Wilson*: "A watermelon is chief of this world's luxuries, king by grace of God over all the fruits of the earth. When one has tasted it, he knows what the angels eat."

Slightly smaller in size, but certainly not in character, cantaloupes are the other most prominent melon variety. Distinguished by a thick, heavenly orange flesh and exquisite aroma, they originated in ancient Persia and spread across the African continent. In the course of time they became especially beloved in Morocco, which remains one of the main global producers today. Matisse's *The Moroccans* (1915–1916), painted following two visits to Tangier in 1912 and 1913, depicts a common street scene: at the entrance of the casbah, hefty melons lie on the pavement. As the torrid heat is felt in the exuberant, highly contrasting colors (Matisse began using black in his compositions after his sojourns in Morocco), looking at the green globes is as refreshing as tasting them would be.

Cantaloupes crossed the Mediterranean and reached Italy in the

WATERMELON, TURKESTAN
Nº 16784
Citrullus lanatus
Los Angeles, Los Angeles County,
California, USA
D. G. Passmore, 1898

14th century. They are named after the town of Cantalupo (roughly translatable as "howl of the wolf"), once a Papal county seat on the Sabine Hills, north of Rome. There they were first cultivated before spreading across the rest of Europe and emerging as a favorite in aristocratic circles. Pope Paul II was famously deeply fond of the fruit—a weakness that was, perhaps, his undoing. In 1470, the pope's cook published a book in which he suggested melons should be eaten as appetizers and in small quantities, since consuming a large portion on a full stomach could have dangerous repercussions. The following year, one story goes, Paul II devoured two whole melons in one sitting and died of severe indigestion. One need only imagine the fruits' superbly sweet, intensely fragrant, vibrantly hued pulp to understand, even to sympathize, with the pope's gluttonous end.

Citrullus lanatus
Cucumis melo

No. 88882.
"Tom Watson."
Dr. Shoemaker.
Bought in Center Market.
1/3ᵈ size.

R. C. Steadman.
7-1-'16
6-28-'16

WATERMELON, TOM WATSON
№ 88882
Citrullus lanatus
Location unknown
R. C. Steadman, 1916

The above and following illustrations are noted to be one-third of the size of the original specimen.

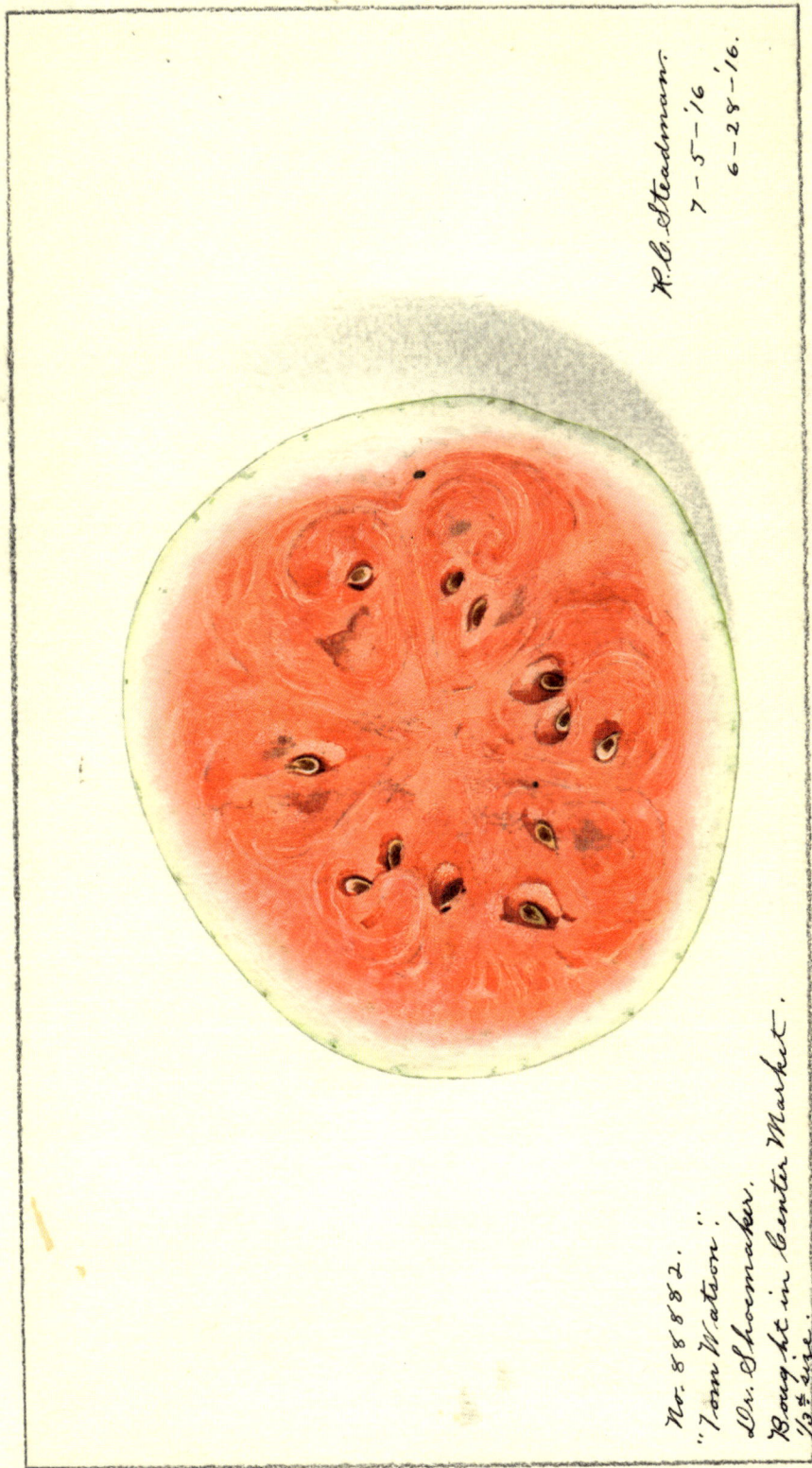

R. C. Steadman.
7 - 5 - '16.
6 - 28 - '16.

Nr. 88882.
"Tom Watson".
Dr. Shoemaker.
Bought in Center Market.
½ size.

WATERMELON, TOM WATSON
Nº 88882a
Citrullus lanatus
Location unknown
R. C. Steadman, 1916

The Tom Watson is one of the oldest varieties of watermelon. It is popular with cultivators for its resilience in shipping over long distances. Long and cylindrical, its skin is tough, elastic, and light veined but deep green in color, and the fruit's flesh is distinguished by its firm, juicy texture and rich red tint.

Referred to botanically as a "pepo," a melon is, in fact, a kind of berry. Melons have a sweet, pulpy flesh that thrives in hot, dry growing conditions, enjoying 60°F nights and 80°F days without frost. The fruit, on average, takes around 120 days to reach maturity, ripening from the inside.

Melons are consumed mostly in the summer months, and are most popular in and around the areas where they are grown. Buying melons locally, especially in the Southern states, increases the chance of the fruit being sweet, fragrant, and refreshing.

Melons are heavy—according to Guinness World Records, the world's heaviest watermelon weighed an impressive 159 kg (350.5 lb). They are also extremely fragile—beneath a melon's tough rind, the flesh consists of balloon-like cells, turgid with juice that's between 90 and 95 percent water, and so are very easily burst, resulting in mushy, spongy, soft flesh and miserable disappointment. This explains why the USDA collection holds so few watercolors of melons, as only a handful of specimens survived the perilous journey to the artists' studios.

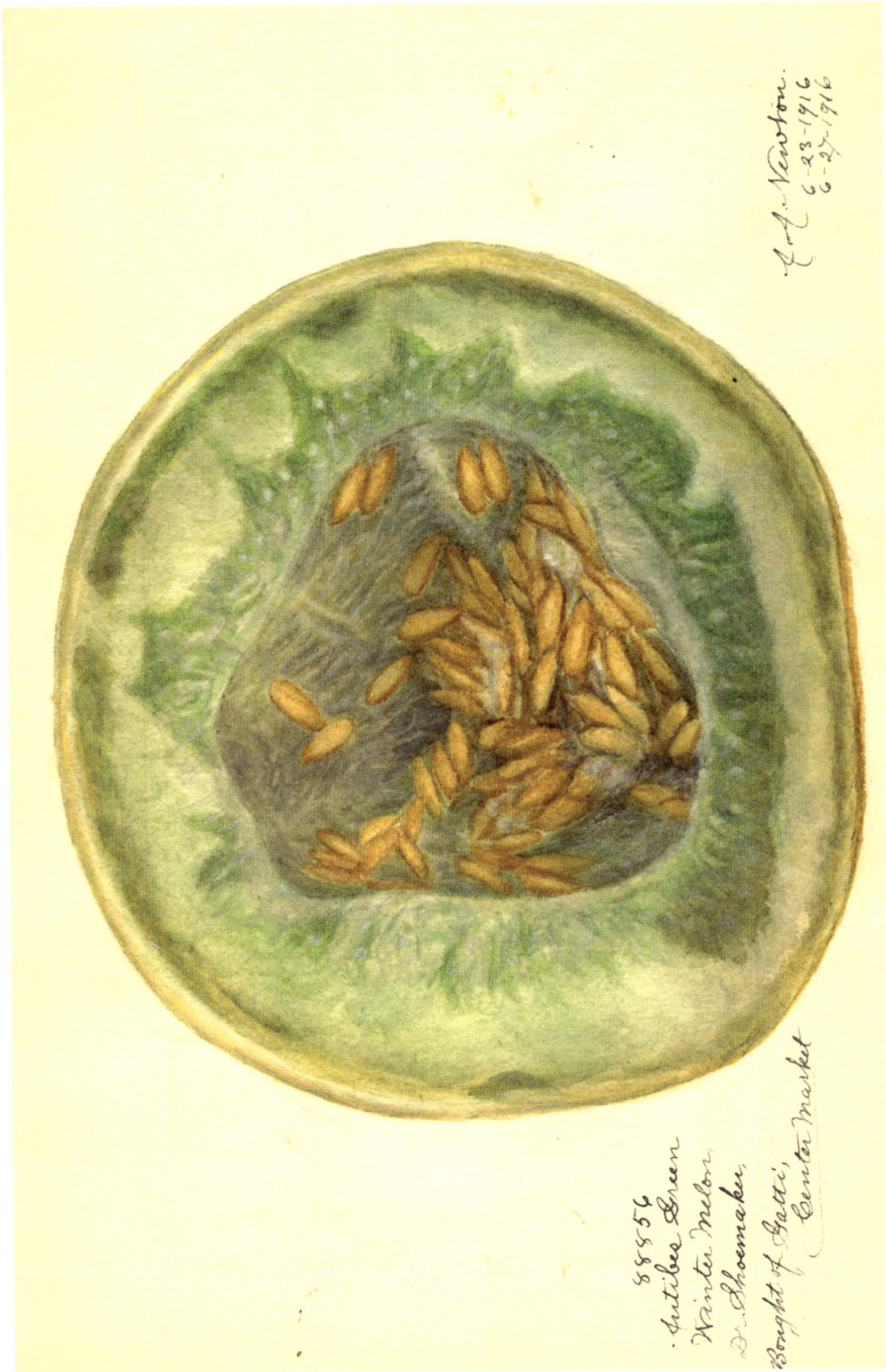

MELON, ANTIBES GREEN
Nº 88856
Cucumis melo
Location unknown
A. A. Newton, 1916

This specimen was bought in the Central Market of Gatti. The Honey Dew melon is prized as one of the sweetest varieties of the fruit. It is noted for its creamy yellow rind and green pale flesh. In Ancient Egypt, the honey melon was regarded as sacred and reserved for the elite, with Cleopatra, Napoleon Bonaparte, and Pope Paul II all known to be enamored of its sweetness.

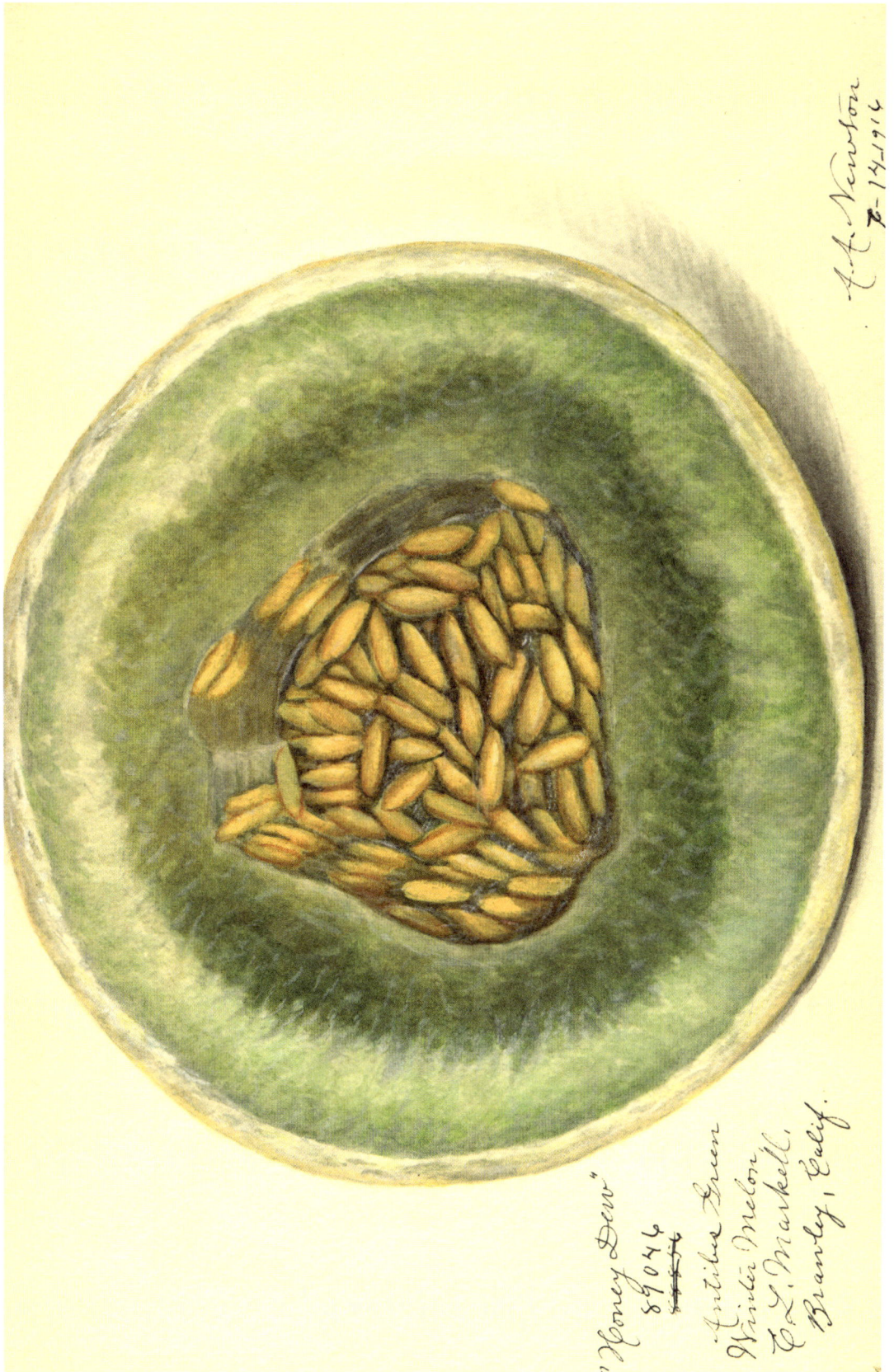

MELON, HONEY DEW
Nº 89046
Cucumis melo
Brawley, Imperial County,
California, USA
A. A. Newton, 1916

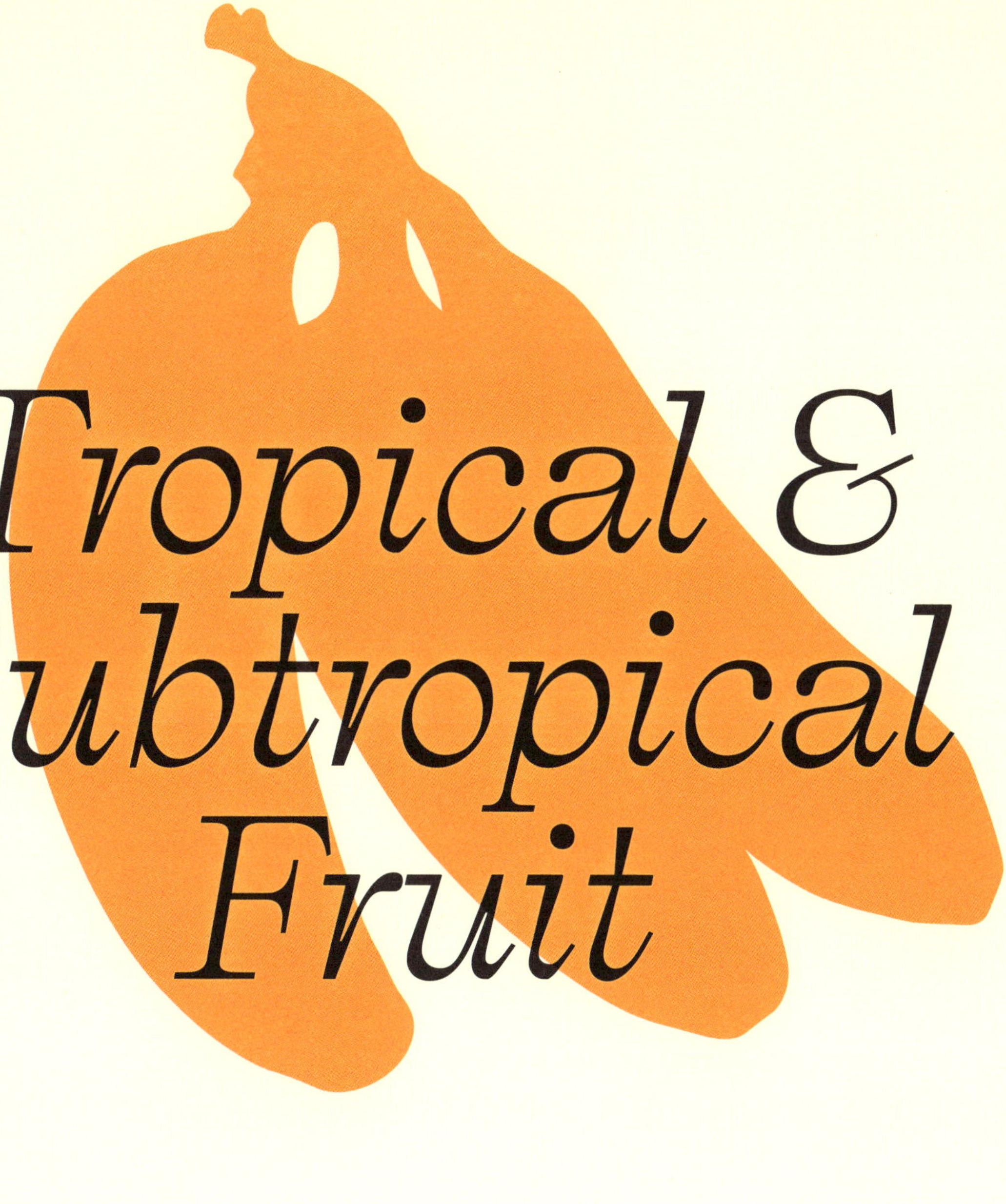

Tropical & Subtropical Fruit

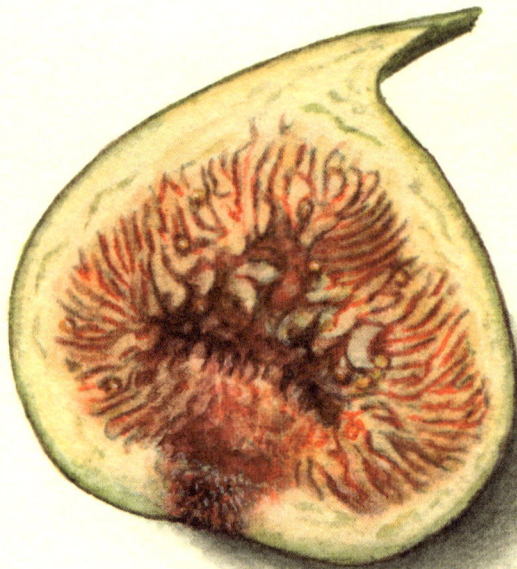

84817.

nameless

L. E. Hall

Hattiesburg,

Miss.

Mary J. Arnold

*T*ropical—the word evokes faraway lands and torrid climates. While many varieties of tropical and subtropical fruit have become culinary staples in North America following their introduction by fruit explorers, many more remain unfamiliar, their flavors and characteristics a matter of speculation to most. Whether encountering them at a local farmers' market or by chance in a remote place, tasting a fruit for the first time is one of life's finest small pleasures, one that can rouse a multitude of feelings—from a sense of wonder akin to new discoveries made in childhood to an unsettling nostalgia for the unfamiliar, such as the state described by American poet Mary Oliver in her 1986 sonnet "The Mango":

> One evening
> I met the mango.
> [...]
> When I began to eat
> things happened.
> All through the sweetness
> I heard voices,
> men and women talking about something—
> another country, and trouble.
> It wasn't my language, but I understood enough.

Unfortunately, room is too scarce to address all of the magnificent fruits depicted in the following pages. Each is blessed with unique and wonderful traits, and with equally engaging histories, but two in particular stand out in having stories that stand comparison to any of the world's most famous human figures—the spectacular pomegranate and the ethereal fig.

With its graceful, divinely rounded shape and copious, flamboyantly crimson seeds, the pomegranate is at the heart of one of Greek mythology's most extraordinary stories: that of Persephone. Persephone lived peacefully in a world of permanent summer with her mother, Demeter, the Olympian goddess of harvest. But one day Hades, god of the underworld, burst from a cleft in the earth and abducted her. In the depths of grief, Demeter neglected the earth, and nothing grew. Meanwhile, Persephone was told she would be released as long as she did not taste any of the food from the underworld. She complied, but when Hades offered her six pomegranate seeds, she could not resist, and ate them. A compromise was found eventually—Persephone was allowed return to the earth, which began to bloom again, but for only six months of each year—one for each seed. For the remainder of the year, she has to retire to the underworld with Hades, causing the climate to grow colder and the earth infertile: this is how the seasons came to be.

So the pomegranate might have caused the seasons; as for the fig, it may have caused a war. The Persian king Xerxes the Great had a passion for figs, especially those from Attica—the Black Royal variety. Known as Greece's finest figs, their pulp was succulent and their skin dark burgundy. According to the ancient historian Herodotus, Xerxes sought to conquer the Attic peninsula so he could enjoy its fresh figs every day, and so began the second Persian invasion of Greece. After Xerxes and his army suffered a

FIGS, NAMELESS
N° 84817
Ficus
Hattiesburg, Forrest County,
Mississippi, USA
M. D. Arnold, 1915

269

disastrous defeat in the Battle of Salamis in 480 BCE, he had figs from Attica served to him after every meal, to remind him that he did not possess the land where this marvelous fruit grew.

Xerxes was not alone in his infatuation with the fruit: it seems figs were a favorite of several ancient dynasts. Cleopatra, the last active ruler of the Ptolemaic Kingdom of Egypt, adored figs so much she famously ordered them for her last meal. Following the Roman Republic's conquest of Egypt in 30 BCE, Cleopatra committed suicide to avoid the humiliation of being taken prisoner by Octavian. Plutarch chronicles how Cleopatra approached her suicide almost as a ritual, involving bathing and a poisonous snake concealed in a basket of figs: "It is said that the asp was brought with those figs and leaves and lay hidden beneath them, for thus Cleopatra had given orders, that the reptile might fasten itself upon her body without her being aware of it. But when she took away some of the figs and saw it, she said: 'There it is, you see,' and baring her arm she held it out for the bite." As Cleopatra became a cultural icon over the centuries, her death became as talked of and romanticized as her life. One of the most notable depictions of the scene, *Cleopatra* (1640) by the Italian Baroque painter Guido Reni, shows the queen holding the asp, gazing at the sky beatifically as she prepares to receive the fatal bite. Beside her lies a basket of fleshy, dark, enticing figs.

Actinidia deliciosa
Adansonia digitata
Aegle marmelos
Ananas comosus
Annona cherimola
Annona reticulata
Annona squamosa
Blighia sapida
Carica papaya
Casimiroa edulis
Chrysophyllum cainito
Clausena lansium
Diospyros
Eriobotrya japonica
Eugenia uniflora
Ficus
Garcinia mangostana
Hibiscus sabdariffa
Mammea americana
Mangifera indica
Manilkara zapota
Musa
Passiflora
Persea
Phoenix dactylifera
Pouteria campechiana
Psidium guajava
Punica granatum
Sechium edule
Solanum betaceum
Spondias purpurea
Swinglea glutinosa
Tamarindus indica
Triphasia aurantiola Lour.
Vasconcellea quercifolia

BANANA, POPOULU HAWAII
N° 38188
Musa
Puerto Rico, USA
A. A. Newton, 1907

The meaning of the scientific name for the banana, *Musa sapientum*, is "fruit of the wise man." The fiber of the wise man's fruit is used in some cultures to make fabrics and paper.

BANANA, GUINCOS FINGET
Nº 38393
Musa
Mayaguez, Puerto Rico, USA
A. A. Newton, 1907

Ynjerto

N. 32367.

J. A. McDowell.

Mexico City, Mexico

E. I. Schutt
Oct. 3d 190

BANANA, YENJERTO
Nº 32367
Musa
Mexico City, Mexico
E. I. Schutt, 1904

No. 36498½.
"Dacca"
C. W. Barrett
Subtropical garden
Miami Fla.

E. I. Schutt.
Aug 27 - 1906
" 31. "

BANANA, DACCA
Nº 36498 1/2
Musa
Miami, Dade County,
Florida, USA
E. I. Schutt, 1906

19443 "Paradise"
Musa paradisiaca.
Var. sapientum. E.J.Brown Lemon City Fla.
D.G.Passmore
5.2.1900

BANANA, PARADISE
Nº 19443
Musa
Lemon City, Dade County,
Florida, USA
D. G. Passmore, 1900

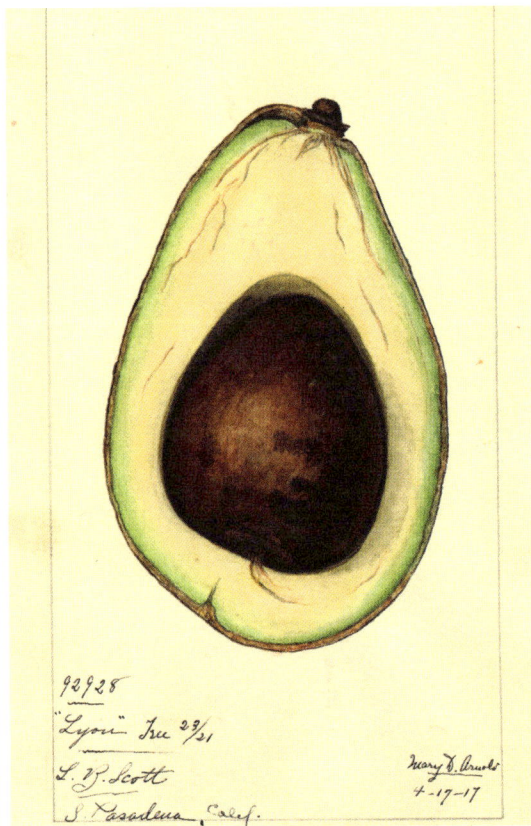

(top left) AVOCADO, BUTLER, Nº 74070, *Persea*, Miami, Dade County, Florida, USA.
M. Strange, 1914. (top right) AVOCADO, BUTLER, Nº 74070a, *Persea*, Miami, Dade County,
Florida, USA. M. Strange, 1914. (bottom left) AVOCADO, PERFECTO, Nº 1590, *Persea*.
Orlando, Orange County, Florida, USA. Artist unknown, 1932. Artificially inoculated in
June, July, August, and September 1932. (bottom right) AVOCADO, LYON, Nº 92928a, *Persea*.
South Pasadena, Los Angeles County, California, USA. M. D. Arnold, 1917.

No. 88451.
"Wagner"
C. F. Wagner.
Hollywood. Calif.

R. C. Steadman.
5-16-'16
5-18-'16

AVOCADO, WAGNER
№ 88451
Persea
Hollywood, Los Angeles County,
California, USA
R. C. Steadman, 1916

No. 83348.
"Taft."
L. B. Scott.
C. P. Taft. Orange, Caly.

R. C. Steadman.
8-21-'17
8-6-'17

AVOCADO, TAFT
№ 83348
Persea
Orange, Orange County,
California, USA
R. C. Steadman, 1917

The Taft variety of avocado originated in 1899 in California and was officially propagated in 1912. The fruit has a broad pear-like shape with a faintly rough skin that bears many yellowish dots. Its flesh is excellent in both flavor and quality.

No. 93348.
Taft.
L. B. Scott.
C. P. Taft. Orange, Caly.

R. C. Steadman.
8 - 10 -'17
8 - 6 -'17

AVOCADO, TAFT
Nº 93348a
Persea
Orange, Orange County,
California, USA
R. C. Steadman, 1917

AVOCADO, THOMPSON
Nº 109049
Persea
Montebello, Los Angeles County,
California, USA
R. C. Steadman, 1927

No. 96804.
Queen.
E. E. Knight.
Guatemala Avocado Nursery.

R. C. Steadman.
6 – 19 – '19
6 – 17 – '19
Yorba Linda, Calif.

AVOCADO, QUEEN
Nº 96804
Persea
Yorba Linda, Orange County,
California, USA
R. C. Steadman, 1919

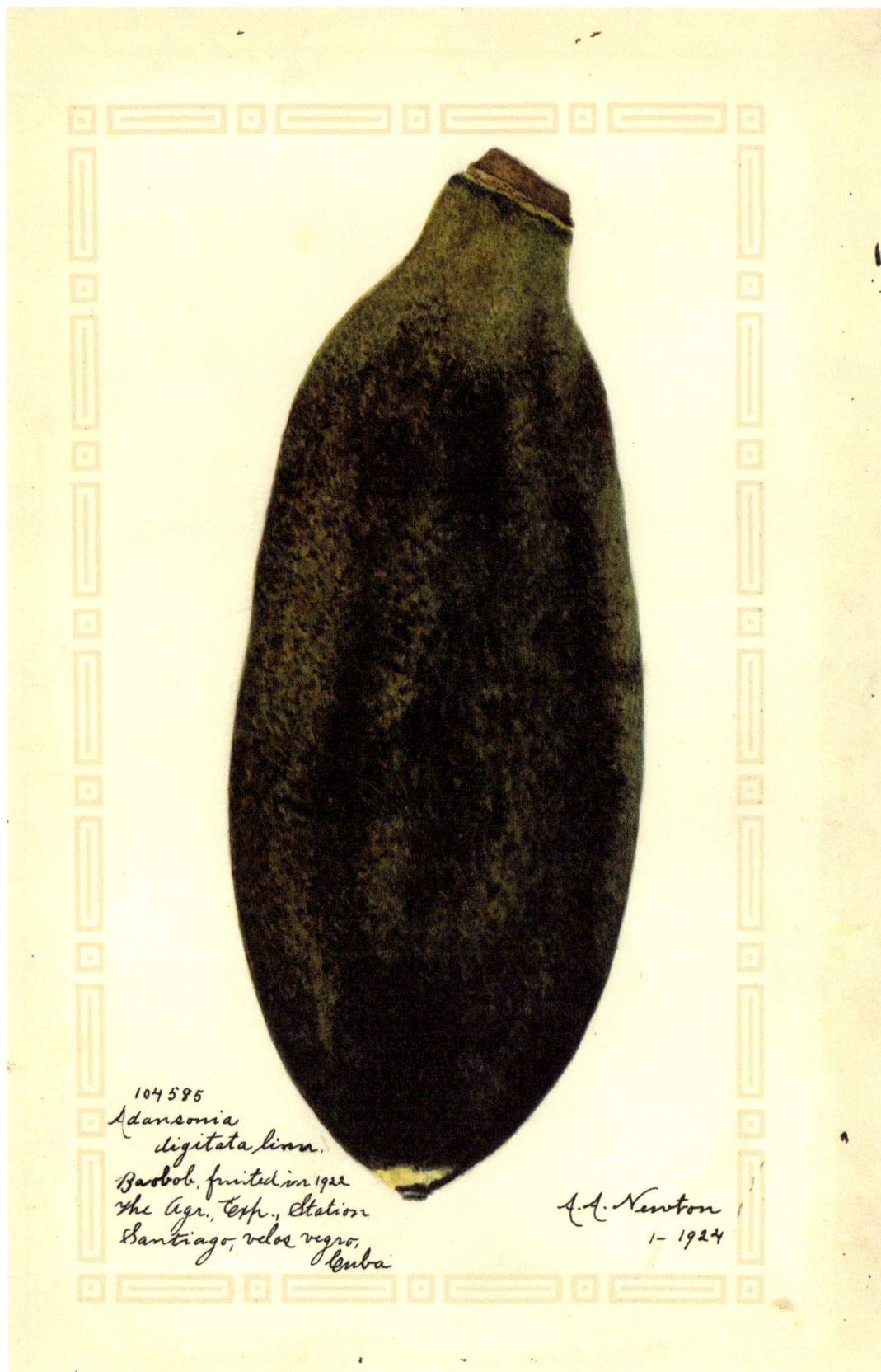

BAOBAB
Nº 104585
Adansonia digitata
Santiago de las Vegas, Havana,
Ciudad de la Habana, Cuba
A. A. Newton, 1924

The baobab tree has been recorded as living for over 3,000 years. When the plant does die, instead of rotting it typically collapses. Some people believe that if you pick one of the flowers from the baobab, you will be eaten by a lion. But, if you drink the water that seeds of the tree have been soaked in, you will be safe from crocodile attacks.

BAOBAB
Nº 104585a
Adansonia digitata
Santiago de las Vegas, Havana,
Ciudad de la Habana, Cuba
A. A. Newton, 1924

No. 95458.
Chayote
from S. P. I.

R. C. Steadman.
4-23-'18
4-18-'18

CHAYOTE
Nº 95458
Sechium edule
Location unknown
R. C. Steadman, 1918

The chayote is known for its cell-regenerative properties, and in contemporary legend it is believed that the fruit was the cause of mummification of people from Colombian in the town of San Bernardo who consumed it in large quantities. Today the well-preserved skin and flesh can still be seen in the remains of the mummies.

CHAYOTE
Nº 49888a
Sechium edule
Santa Barbara, Santa Barbara County,
California, USA
E. I. Schutt, 1910

№ 50539.
Anona reticulata
Peter Bisset.
Nassau.
B. I.

E. I. Schutt
April 13-'11
" 18-'11.

CUSTARD APPLE
Nº 50539
Annona reticulata
Location unknown
E. I. Schutt, 1911

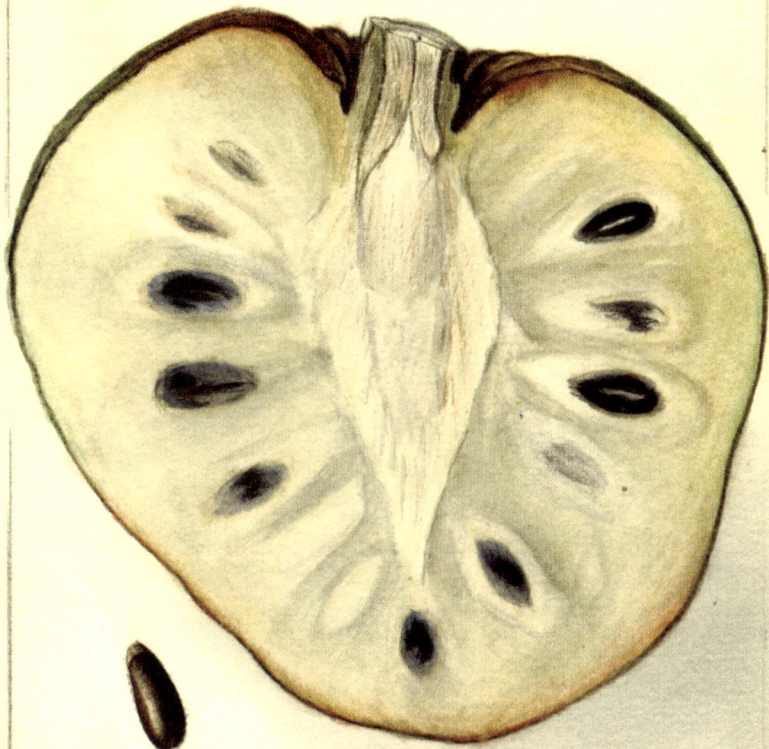

No 50539.
Anona reticulata
Peter Bisset
Nassau.
BS.

E. I. Schutt
April 13-'11
April. 19-'11

CUSTARD APPLE
Nº 50539a
Annona reticulata
Location unknown
E. I. Schutt, 1911

CHERIMOYA, GOLDEN RUSSET
№ 46532
Annona cherimola
Orange, Orange County,
California, USA
E. E. Lower, 1910

The American writer Mark Twain called the cherimoya "the most delicious fruit known to men." Due to its creamy nature, it is eaten with a spoon.

288

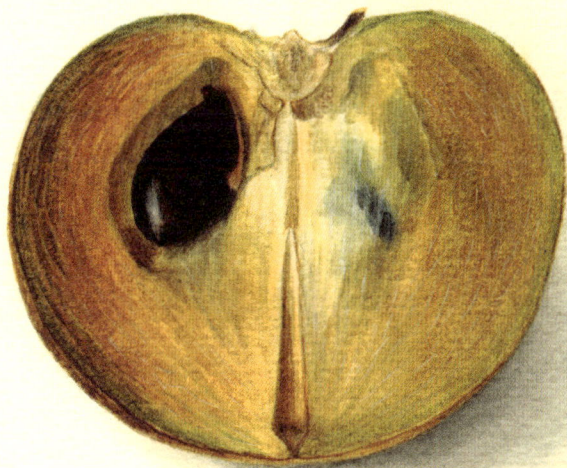

SAPODILLA, Nº 8
Nº 35972
Manilkara zapota
Miami, Dade County,
Florida, USA
A. A. Newton, 1906

The sapodilla plant, which is native to southern Mexico, produces a latex that is the source of a natural chewing gum eaten by the Aztecs, called chicle.

No. 36149.
"Tafilalt"
David Fairchild
Morocco.

E. I. Schutt
June 23 '06

DATE, TAFILALT
Nº 36149
Phoenix dactylifera
Morocco
E. I. Schutt, 1906

It is noted that it is unclear if Tafilalt is the name of the variety or the region in Morocco.

290

The American date industry has its roots in Morocco, where, in 1927, agricultural explorer Walter Tennyson Swingle secured a collection of Medjool date palm offshoots and sent them back to the US.

The date is often depicted as delightfully fat and maple-hued, and has a famously succulent, irresistibly gooey texture. Americans were immediately enamored of the fruit and its connections with what they saw as the exotic Orient. They had recently fallen head over heels for the glamour of films such as Rudolph Valentino's *The Sheik*, and had long adored the book *One Thousand and One Nights* (also known as *The Arabian Nights' Entertainment*). For growers at the time, the date's cultural connections made it powerfully attractive as a crop.

The growth in the sweet fruit's popularity transformed the Coachella Valley into an oasis of mimicked pyramids, camel rides, and harems that were all created to draw crowds to see the romantic produce the land was now producing.

Sweet Sop
Anona squamosa
from G. T. King
Villa City Florida
D. G. Passmore
10. 22. 92

SWEETSOP
No 4440
Annona squamosa
Villa City, Lake County,
Florida, USA
D. G. Passmore, 1892

SWEETSOP, ANONA № 5
№ 46712
Annona squamosa
Santa Barbara, Santa Barbara
County, California, USA
D. G. Passmore, 1910

43936
Mammee apple
Sub-Tropical Exp. Sta.
Miami, Dade Co Fla.

E.I. Schutt.
July 27 '09
Aug. 9 '09

MAMMEE APPLE
№ 43936
Mammea americana
Miami, Dade County,
Florida, USA
E. I. Schutt, 1909

294

"Tamarind"

40857
Wm. Fremd
Palm Beach,
Dade Co. Fla.
5/1/08

A. A. Newton
5/6/08

INDIAN TAMARIND
N⁰ 40857
Tamarindus indica
Palm Beach, Palm Beach County,
Florida, USA
A. A. Newton, 1908

The location was changed from Dade County to Palm Beach County in the archive. The name of the tamarind comes from an Arab expression meaning "date of India." The fruit is so sour that Marco Polo claimed that the Malabar pirates forced their victims to swallow a mixture of tamarind and seawater, causing them to vomit and reveal any pearls they may have swallowed.

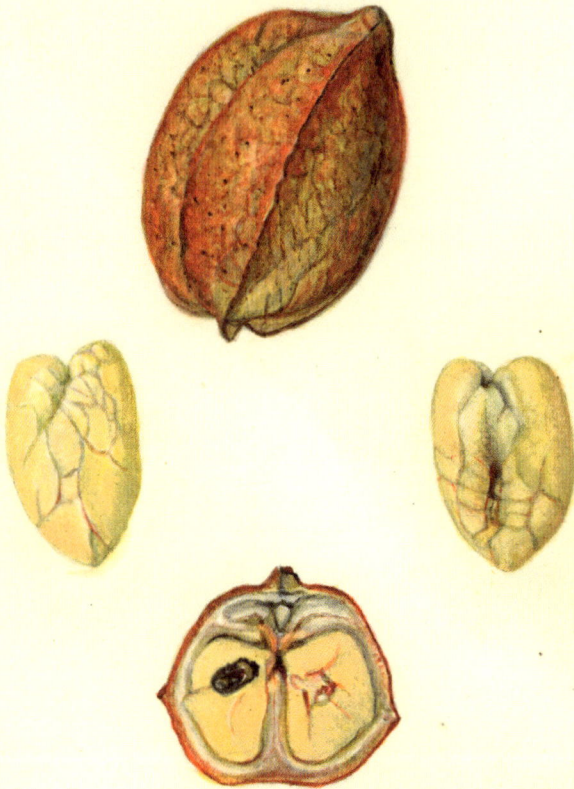

104781
"Cupania Sapida"
Savoury.
native N. Africa
naturalized in W. Ind.
akee tree

A. A. Newton
1-21-1924

AKEE, SAVOURY
Nº 104781
Blighia sapida
West Indies
A. A. Newton, 1924

Blighia (or *Cupania*) *sapida* is native to North Africa and was naturalized in the West Indies.

(top) CANISTEL, MAMMEY, Nº 43681, *Pouteria campechiana*, location unknown. A. A. Newton, 1909. This specimen was bought from Louis P. Gatti by W. A. Taylor, Assistant Chief of the Bureau of Plant Industry, USDA, 1909–1913. *(bottom)* BAEL, Nº 43659 & 43660a, *Aegle marmelos*, Muzaffarpur, Bihar, India. E. I. Schutt, 1909. Indian Bael from the USDA, Shipping Point Inspection.

GUAVA
Nº 00312
Psidium guajava
Tampa, Hillsborough County,
Florida, USA
R. C. Steadman, 1931

The guava was once forbidden in Philippine mythology until
a child prayed to the gods to make the inedible fruit delicious
so that he could share it with a beggar.

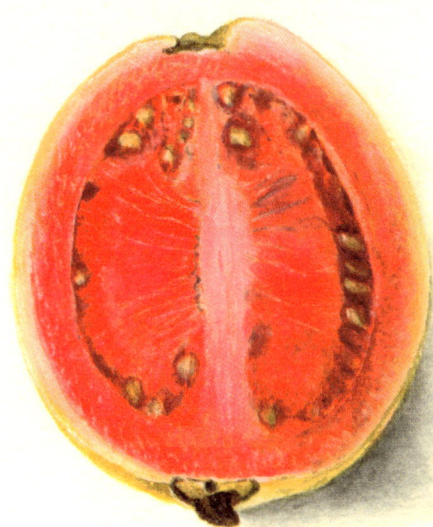

36599
Red Fleshed Guava
& D. Brown
Miami Dade Co.
Fla.

A. A. Newton
Sep. 6-06
7-06

GUAVA, RED FLESHED
Nº 36599
Psidium guajava
Miami, Dade County,
Florida, USA
A. A. Newton, 1906

No. 96797.
Champagne.
C. P. Taft.
Orange, Calif.

R. C. Steadman.
5 - 28 - '19
5 - 24 - '19

LOQUAT, CHAMPAGNE
Nº 96797
Eriobotrya japonica
Orange, Orange County,
California, USA
R. C. Steadman, 1919

The Champagne loquat, which today is frequently misidentified as Early Red, was first introduced into cultivation by C. P. Taft around 1908.

300

19427 Loquat "Advance"
E.J. Jaft
Orange Co. California
D. G. Passmore
4. 18. 1900.

LOQUAT, ADVANCE
Nº 19427
Eriobotrya japonica
Orange, Orange County,
California, USA
D. G. Passmore, 1900

No. 36 983.
Quercifolia
J. W. Riggs
Waterloo
Kingman Co, Kan.

E. I. Schutt
Oct 10 – 1906
" 25 – " –

OAK LEAVED PAPAYA
Nº 36983
Vasconcellea quercifolia
Waterloo, Kingman County,
Kansas, USA
E. I. Schutt, 1906

302

PAPAYA
Nº 56863a
Carica papaya
Location unknown
M. D. Arnold, 1912

This specimen was discovered by David Fairchild. Papayas were first introduced in the 1800s to Hawaii, the only state in the US that grows the fruit commercially. Traditionally consumed in India, Pakistan, and Sri Lanka by women for natural birth control, the papaya is known to have contraceptive properties if eaten in large quantities, even inducing miscarriages in some cases.

46800
"Mangalore"
aston W. Gardner & Co.
Kingston
Jamaica.

A. A. Newton.
5-10-10. 5-13-10

MANGO, MANGALORE
№ 46800
Mangifera indica
Kingston,
Surrey, Jamaica
A. A. Newton, 1910

The mango, an ancient fruit that can be dated back 4,000 years, is said to have caught the eye of Alexander the Great, who brought the fruit back with him from his travels in Greece. It is also said that Emperor Jehangir, the fourth Mughal Emperor, was a admirer of the mango and famously stated that none of the fruits in Kabul could match up to the flavors of its fragrantly sweet flesh.

MANGO, HAYDEN
Nº 103257
Mangifera indica
Miami, Dade County,
Florida, USA
R. C. Steadman, 1923

Studies by J. M. Shull of anthracnose-damaged mangoes *(Mangifera indica)*.
(top left) BENNETT, Nº 604, Miami, Dade County, Florida, USA, 1912. *(top right)* Nº 343, West Palm Beach, Palm Beach County, Florida, USA, 1910. *(bottom left)* FERNANDEZ, Nº 621, West Palm Beach, Palm Beach County, Florida, USA, 1912. *(bottom right)* MULGOBA, Nº 606, Miami, Dade County, Florida, USA, 1912.

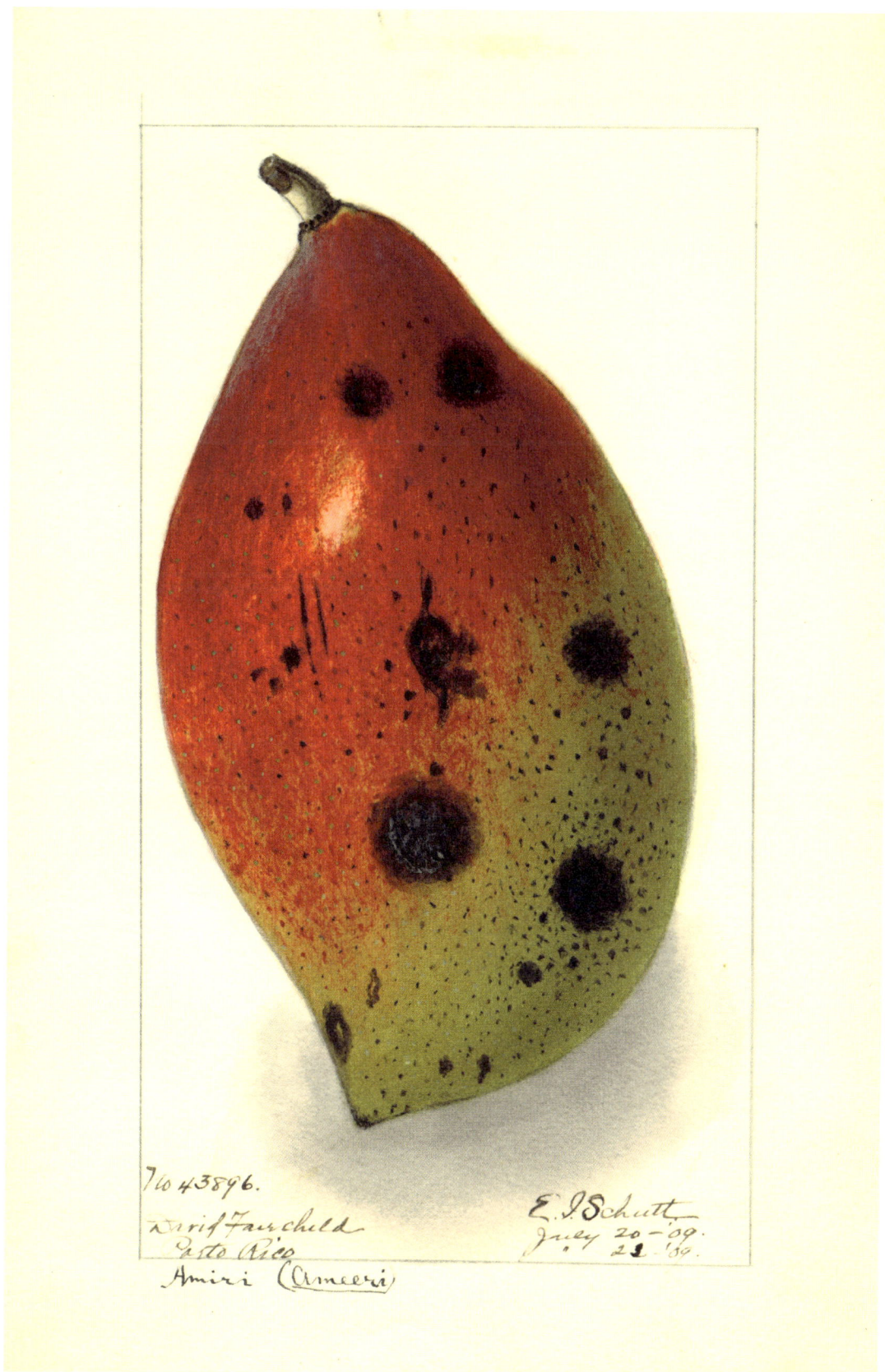

MANGO, AMEERI, AMIRI
Nº 43896
Mangifera indica
Puerto Rico, USA
E. I. Schutt, 1909

This specimen was received from David Fairchild at the USDA, Shipping Point Inspection.

41629
Bergamont Lime
Prof. P. J. Wester
Miami
Dade Co
Fla.   triphasia aurantiola Lour
Elsie E. Lower.
8 - 24 - 08
8 - 31 - 08

LIMEBERRY, BERGAMONT LIME
Nº 41629
Triphasia aurantiola Lour.
Miami, Dade County,
Florida, USA
E. E. Lower, 1908

MANGOSTEEN
Nº 00296
Garcinia mangostana
Location unknown
D. G. Passmore, 1904

The mangosteen's flavor has been described as being similar to a peach, strawberry, or grape—and like an orange the fruit's juicy flesh is characteristically divided into segments. In the 19th century, it was rumored that Queen Victoria had offered £100 to anyone who could bring her a mangosteen fruit.

#19479
Granadilla,
from
E.J. Brown,
5/25-1900 Lemon City, Dade co., Fla.
B. Heiges
6-1-1900

Fruit rotted before section could be painted.
Strawberry rich. June - 1900

PASSIFLORA
Nº 19479
Passiflora
Lemon City, Dade County,
California, USA
B. Heiges, 1900

This fruit is noted to have rotted before a section could be painted.

310

PERSIMMON, YEDO ICHI
N⁰ 00018
Diospyros
Jewella,
Louisiana, USA
W. H. Prestele, 1888

Notes on the illustration state that this specimen was probably the variety Goshio-Hira rather than Yedo Ichi. It was also received from New Orleans not Lemon City, and drawn from nature by W. H. Prestele.

PERSIMMON, SHAKUMI
Nº 107214
Diospyros
Chico, Butte County,
California, USA
R. C. Steadman, 1925

312

PERSIMMON, KUROKUMA
Nº 106202
Diospyros
Palo Alto, Santa Clara County,
California, USA
R. C. Steadman, 1925

Studies of persimmons (*Diospyros*).
(*top left*) TSURU, Nº 00026, Live Oak, Florida, USA. Artist unknown, 1888. Specimen noted as not typical. (*top right*) TAMOPAN, Nº 1304, Live Oak, Florida, USA. J. M. Shull, 1923. Specimen collected on 19 June 1923. (*bottom*) ZENGI, Nº 00035, Location unknown. Artist unknown, n.d.

PERSIMMON, TSURU KO KO
Nº 86313
Diospyros
Augusta, Richmond County,
Georgia, USA
A. A. Newton, 1915

50/63
"Clausena Whampi"
C. F. Franceschi.
Santa Barbara
Santa Barbara Co.
Calif.

Elsie E. Lower.
1 - 27 - 1911
1 - 31 - 1911

WAMPEE, WHAMPI
Nº 50163
Clausena lansium
Santa Barbara, Santa Barbara County,
California, USA
E. E. Lower, 1911

316

23015 Tree Tomato
"Cyphomandra betacea"
(Solanum fragrans, Hook.)
Elmer Stearns.
10/14/01 Los Angeles, Los Angeles Co., Calif.
B. Heiges
10/24/01

TREE TOMATO
Nº 23015
Solanum betaceum
Los Angeles, Loss Angeles County,
California, USA
B. Heiges, 1901

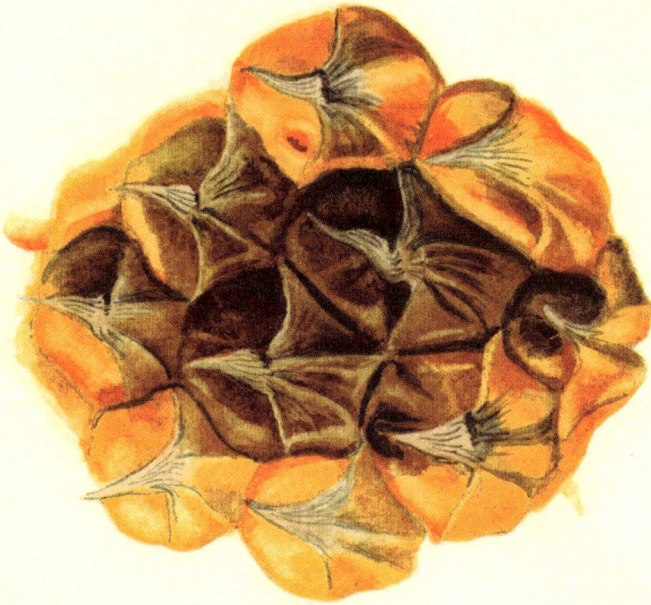

PINEAPPLE
Nº 1177
Ananas comosus
Puerto Rico, USA
J. M. Shull, 1919

Physiological or mechanical damage shown in illustration not specified. Ancient civilizations such as the Mayans and the Aztecs were largely familiar with the yellow-fleshed pineapple fruit. In 1493 Christopher Columbus successfully brought the fruit to Europe.

PINEAPPLE
Nº 1155
Ananas comosus
Cuba
J. M. Shull, 1919

This specimen was subject to a secondary inoculation with bacteria. The damage shown is noted as *Thielaviopsis*.

POMEGRANATE
Nº 00313
Punica granatum
Location unknown
A. A. Newton, n.d.

The Latin name for the pomegranate, *Punica*, comes from the Roman name for Carthage, an ancient city in Northern Africa. In Greek mythology, the pomegranate was considered the "fruit of the dead" after Hades, the god of the underworld, used the seeds of the fruit to trick Persephone into returning to the underworld for a few months every year.

320

"Wonderful"
Sacaton
in storage about three months
Stored in cold storage plant
Arlington Va.   A. A. Newton
                                        1-10-1920

POMEGRANATE, WONDERFUL
Nº 1101920
Punica granatum
Rosslyn, Arlington County,
Virginia, USA
A. A. Newton, 1920

37510
Rozelle
Mrs E.S. Rolfs
Miami
Dade Co. Fla.

D.G.Passmore
12.2.06
12.4.06

ROSELLE
Nº 37510
Hibiscus sabdariffa
Miami, Dade County,
Florida, USA
D. G. Passmore, 1906

The roselle grows naturally in Guinea, the Antilles, and throughout Central America.

322

SURINAM CHERRY
Nº 19425
Eugenia uniflora
Lemon City, Dade County,
Florida, USA
D. G. Passmore, 1900

42696
Actinidia, Kolomikta?
R.J. Fairchild,
S.P.I.

A.A. Newton
10-22-08
10-27-'08

KIWIFRUIT
Nº 42696
Actinidia deliciosa
Location unknown
A. A. Newton, 1908

This specimen was received from David Fairchild at the USDA, Shipping Point Inspection. The kiwi is one of today's most popular fruits, eaten for its soft and juicy texture and flavor that can be described as a mixture of peaches, strawberries, and melons.

31723
Scarlet Plum
Prof P. H. Rolfs
Miami
Dade Co. Fla.

D. G. Passmore
July 1st 1904

RED MOMBIN, SCARLET PLUM
Nº 31723
Spondias purpurea
Miami, Dade County,
Florida, USA
D. G. Passmore, 1904

This variety is alternatively called Purple Mombin.

No. 40872   E. I. Schutt.
Crysophyllum Monospyreum.   May 4 - 1908.
J. B. Donnelly.   May 13 - 08.
Palm Beach
Dade, Co. Fla.

STAR APPLE
Nº 40872
Chrysophyllum cainito
Palm Beach County,
Florida, USA
E. I. Schutt, 1908

The location was changed from Dade County to Palm Beach
County in the archive. The star apple is part of the Sapotaceae
family and a relative of both the mamey and green sapote.

326

TABOG
Nº 43247
Swinglea glutinosa
Manila, Philippines
D. G. Passmore, 1909

46943
White Sapote
(Casimiroa edulis)
Mr. Biscett
Int. Tropical Garden
Miami, Fla.

Elsie E. Lower.
6-11-1910
6-20-1910

WHITE SAPOTE
N° 46943
Casimiroa edulis
Miami, Dade County,
Florida, USA
E. E. Lower, 1910

328

Calimyrna Fig
J. C. Roeding's
Fresno. Cal.
Series 12

Experimental Shipment.
Aug. 27. 1912
Rec'd N.Y. Sept 13. 1912

E. Lower Pomeroy.

FIG, CALIMYRNA
Nº 00294
Ficus
Fresno, Fresno County,
California, USA
E. E. Lower, 1912

E. E. Lower signed this watercolor with her married name, Pomeroy.
The fig dates back some 6,000 years when it is known to have grown in
ancient Egypt to be eaten as a treat by Cleopatra, who prized the fruit
for its high sugar content that gives it such a beautifully sweet flavor.
The tree of the fig is pollinated by its own distinct species of fig wasps,
and it intriguingly flowers from inside of the fruit, meaning there are no
blossoms on fig trees.

FIG, ROYAL BLACK
Nº 48925
Ficus
Washington DC, USA
E. E. Lower, 1912

It is noted on the illustration folder that Mr Tassa grew brown, white, and black fig varieties that were brought back from Italy in 1894 by his brother. The black fig is similar to that in this drawing.

FIG, SILVER
Nº 50981
Ficus
Cape Charles, Northampton County,
Virginia, USA
M. D. Arnold, 1911

The fig plants in fruit that were seen at Cape Charles at the
time were locally known as Silver or Silver Leaf. They were
regarded by the horticulturist Ira J. Condit as being
Magnolia, or more properly the true Brunswick from early
horticultural literature.

Nuts & Miscellaneous

333

32578

Stuart.

Stuart–Robson
Pecan Co.,
Ocean Springs
Jackson Co.,
Miss.

10/13/04

B. Heiges

10/21/04

Healthful, dense, hearty, festive, delicate—nuts are perhaps the most peculiar of fruits. It should be made clear straight away that only a few nuts are fruits in the botanical sense: pomologically, a nut is a fruit characterized by a rigid shell and edible seed (such as the chestnut), while in vernacular usage, the term covers also the seeds of drupe fruits—among them walnuts, almonds, and pecans, as well as the peanut, which is actually a legume.

In the historical Aquitaine region of France, archaeologists have excavated fossilized shells of roasted walnuts dating to the Neolithic era—some 8,000 years ago—meaning walnuts are the first nuts known to have been eaten by humans. This seed's popularity has endured over the ages—it was particularly popular during the period of the Roman empire. The god Jupiter feasted on walnuts while he lived among mortals before retiring to the sky. And so the nut's botanical name *Juglans* derives from Jupiter's alias, Jove, and the Latin for nut, *glans*. The walnut's distinctive brain-like shape and creased shell has also inspired artists over many centuries, often as embodiments of abundance and potency. The famous mosaic trompe l'œil known as the "unswept floor" in Hadrian's villa in Tivoli includes such a depiction: among a plethora of scraps and remains of a lush banquet appears a mouse beside a halved walnut.

The chestnut is no less emblematic, and would be worth mentioning for its delightful life cycle alone, in which the seed, upon maturity, gracefully falls to the ground ensconced in its verdant, spiked carapace. But the tree itself is as iconic as the fruit it bears, and has emerged as a figure of justice and honesty in folklore. Such a tale involves the largest and oldest known tree, the Hundred Horse Chestnut on the eastern slope of Mount Etna in Sicily, which is believed to be between 2,000 and 4,000 years old. The tree's epithet stems from a 16th-century legend in which Joanna of Aragon, the Queen of Naples, found herself caught in a severe thunderstorm on a visit to the volcano and famously sheltered under the 200-foot-wide tree, along with her 100 mounted knights, until the sky cleared.

Chestnuts have been a staple food in Mediterranean countries for centuries, and during the year-end celebration season in Northern Europe are to be found being roasted and sold in the streets. This was a popular tradition in North America also, until a fungus wiped out nearly all the chestnut trees in the early 1900s—today, chestnuts are imported to America, most of them from Italy. Their exquisite, generous, and starchy flesh makes them a cherished ingredient in gourmet confections worldwide. In Southern France, *marrons glacés* (chestnuts candied and glazed in syrup) are savored at Christmas. Behind their creation lies the story of a man's mission to rescue his hometown from hardship and the astounding artistry and resilience of the town's female citizens. In 1882, *pébrine* (pepper disease) vastly reduced the silkworm population and caused the collapse of the economy in Ardèche, which was then largely reliant on sericulture (silk farming). Clément Faugier, an engineer from the village

PECAN, STUART
N° 32578
Carya illinoinensis
Ocean Springs, Jackson County,
Mississippi, USA
B. Heiges, 1904

335

of Privas, built the first factory with the technology to produce *marrons glacés* on an industrial scale. Still, of the 20 steps required in their manufacture, 11 were too intricate for machines and had to be done by hand. Many female laborers left jobless by the silk crisis were employed in the workshop. It is said the *marrons glacés* from Privas are so fine by virtue of the delicacy of these women's fingers, whose skill had been honed over centuries of working with silk. To this day, the Clément Faugier brand continues to specialize in chestnut *gourmandises*, such as the renowned *crème de marrons*.

Curiously, a similar situation involving another nut was evolving at the same time across the Atlantic. The boll weevil, a beetle that feeds on cotton buds and flowers, entered the United States from Mexico in 1892, and by the mid-1920s the entire cotton industry in North America had been devastated by the pest. Encouraged by the pioneering agricultural scientist George Washington Carver, cotton farmers began harvesting peanuts instead. This legume became a staple in the national diet, and several food corporations turned to producing peanut butter (now best known for its ketchup, Heinz made its early reputation with this product). Considered the father of the peanut industry, Carver discovered over 300 culinary and cosmetic uses for the legume, though contrary to popular belief he did not invent the quintessentially American spread. What remains true, however, is that neither *marrons glacés* nor peanut butter might have existed were it not for invasive pests.

Anacardium occidentale
Arachis
Carya
Carya illinoinensis
Caryocar nuciferum
Castanea
Ceratonia siliqua L.
Corylus
Juglans
Juglans ailantifolia
Juglans nigra
Juglans regia
Macadamia ternifolia
Myristica fragrans
Olea europaea
Opuntia
Pinus pinea
Terminalia catappa

ENGLISH WALNUT, PERSIAN WALNUT
N° 40806
Juglans regia
Burlington, Burlington County,
New Jersey, USA
E. I. Schutt, 1908

Substitute Plate VIII

E. E. Risien, San Saba, Texas.

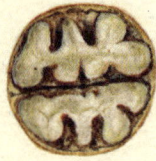

32626 - San Saba.

A. M. Sobral, Logan, St. James Parish, La.

30229. Centennial.

Stuart Pecan Co., Ocean Springs, Jackson Co., Miss.

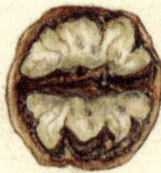

30766 - Jewett

B. M. Young, Morgan City, St. Marys Parish, La.

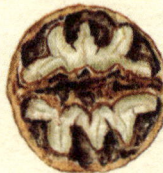

30613 - Frotscher.

Chas. E. Pabst, Ocean Springs, Jackson Co., Miss.

30581 - Pabst.

B. Heiges 1904

PECAN VARIETIES.

PECAN
Nº 32626, 30229, 30766, 30613 & 30581
Carya illinoinensis
Ocean Springs, Jackson County,
Mississippi, USA
B. Heiges, 1904

The San Saba variety (No. 32626) was received from E. E. Risen, San Saba Texas; the Centennial variety (No. 30229) was received from A. M. Sobral, Logan, Louisiana; the Jewett variety (No. 30766) was received from the Stuart Peacan Company, Ocean Springs, Mississippi; the Frotscher variety (No. 30613) was received from B. M. Young, Morgan City, Louisiana; the Pabst variety (No. 30581) was received from C. E. Pabst, Ocean Springs, Mississippi.

Plate 3

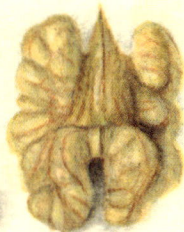

50083

Treyve

49336

Prince

50074

Concord

49867

Wilty

A. A. Newton
4-22-11

WALNUT
No 50083, 49336, 50074 & 49867
Juglans
Location unknown
A. A. Newton, 1911

This illustration shows the following varieties: Treyve (No. 50083), Prince (No. 49336), Concord (No. 50074), and Wilty (No. 49867). It is noted that these four varieties received a lot of attention from growers in the more northern walnut-growing areas of the Pacific Coast.

WALNUT
Nº 470a
Juglans
Jeanerette,
Louisiana, USA
J. M. Shull, 1911

Damage to the twigs is noted as bacteriosis (*Pseudomonas juglandis*). Walnuts in the early 1900s were harvested by hand, when people would use long poles and heavy mallets to knock the nuts off the trees. In more recent years, technology developments have allowed growers to use machinery to harvest the nut in larger quantities more quickly.

BLACK WALNUT
Nº 40850
Juglans nigra
White Pine, Jefferson County,
Tennessee, USA
A. A. Newton, 1908

This illustration is signed by J. C. Clark, a member of the Bureau of Entomology and Plant Quarantine at the USDA. In the past the US Air Force used ground-up walnut shells to clean parts of their aircraft—this was common practice until a Chinook helicopter tragically crashed as a result of the nut's grit clogging up the machinery.

31582
C. B. Gibbins
East Ipswich, Queensland,
Australia

D. G. Passmore
6.3.1904

Queensland Nut (Macadamia ternifolia)

MACADAMIA
Nº 31582
Macadamia ternifolia
Ipswich,
Queensland, Australia
D. G. Passmore, 1904

The location's name was changed from East Ipswich to Ipswich in the archive. The macadamia nut is native to Australia and gets its name from the Scottish-born physician and chemist John Macadam. Macadam during his career was known for his efforts in promoting the nut's cultivation in Australia.

No. 98380.
Souari Nut.
A. J. Simmonds
Los Angeles, Calif.

R. G. Steadman.
6-30-'20.

PEKEA NUT, SOUARI NUT
Nº 98380
Caryocar nuciferum
Los Angeles, Los Angeles County,
California, USA
R. C. Steadman, 1920

Caryocar nuciferum is a fruit tree native to the Amazon region.

32547
"Delmas"
A. G. Delmas
Scranton, Jackson Co., Miss.
10/13/04

B. Heiges
10/27/04

HICKORY, DELMAS
№ 32547
Carya
Pascagoula, Jackson County,
Mississippi, USA
B. Heiges, 1904

According to the archive, the location of Pascagoula was
formerly known as Scranton.

46316
Tropical Almond
Terminalia Catappa
J. Yates Peck
Miami. Dade Co. Fla

D. G. Passmore
2.12.1910
2.21.1909

TROPICAL ALMOND
N° 46316
Terminalia catappa
Miami, Dade County,
Florida, USA
D. G. Passmore, 1910

Terminalia catappa, commonly called the tropical almond, gets its name from the Latin word *terminus*, which refers to a Roman god said to have presided over boundaries and frontiers. Here, however, it refers more directly to the rosette of leaves at the end of the plant's branches.

94251
Chinquapin
Chestnut
Dr. Van Fleet
Bell Sta —
Md.

Mary D. Arnold
10-27-17

CHESTNUT
№ 94251
Castanea
Bell Station, Maryland, USA
M. D. Arnold, 1917

This specimen is noted as the Chinquapin chestnut variety. It is also noted that there is no Bell Station in Maryland but that there is one in Alabama.

346

Yearbook, U.S. Dept. of Agriculture. 1912.

Plate VIII

No. 65788.
Boone
Geo. N. Endicott
Villa Ridge
Illinois.

E. I. Schutt.
Oct 8 - 13
Oct 14 - 13.

Boone Chestnut.

CHESTNUT, BOONE
Nº 65788
Castanea
Villa Ridge, Pulaski County,
Illinois, USA
E. I. Schutt, 1913

This watercolor is a mock-up of Plate VIII in the *Yearbook of Agriculture 1913*. The oldest and largest acorn tree recorded was the Castagno dei Cento Cavalli or the Hundred-Horse Chestnut, found just 8 km (5 miles) from Mount Etna in Sicily, Italy. With a circumference of over 190 ft, the tree is believed to be 2,000 to 4,000 years old, and take its name from when a queen and her 100 knights took shelter under its branches during a storm.

347

No. 88696.
Cashew Nuts.
E. D. Vosbury
Miami, Fla.

6-13-'16
6-12-'16

— R. C. Steadman

CASHEW NUT
Nº 88696
Anacardium occidentale
Miami, Dade County,
Florida, USA
R. C. Steadman, 1916

The name of the cashew nut is derived from the Portuguese name for the fruit of the nut's tree, *caju*, a name that itself comes from the Tupian word *acajú*, literally translated as "nut that produces itself."

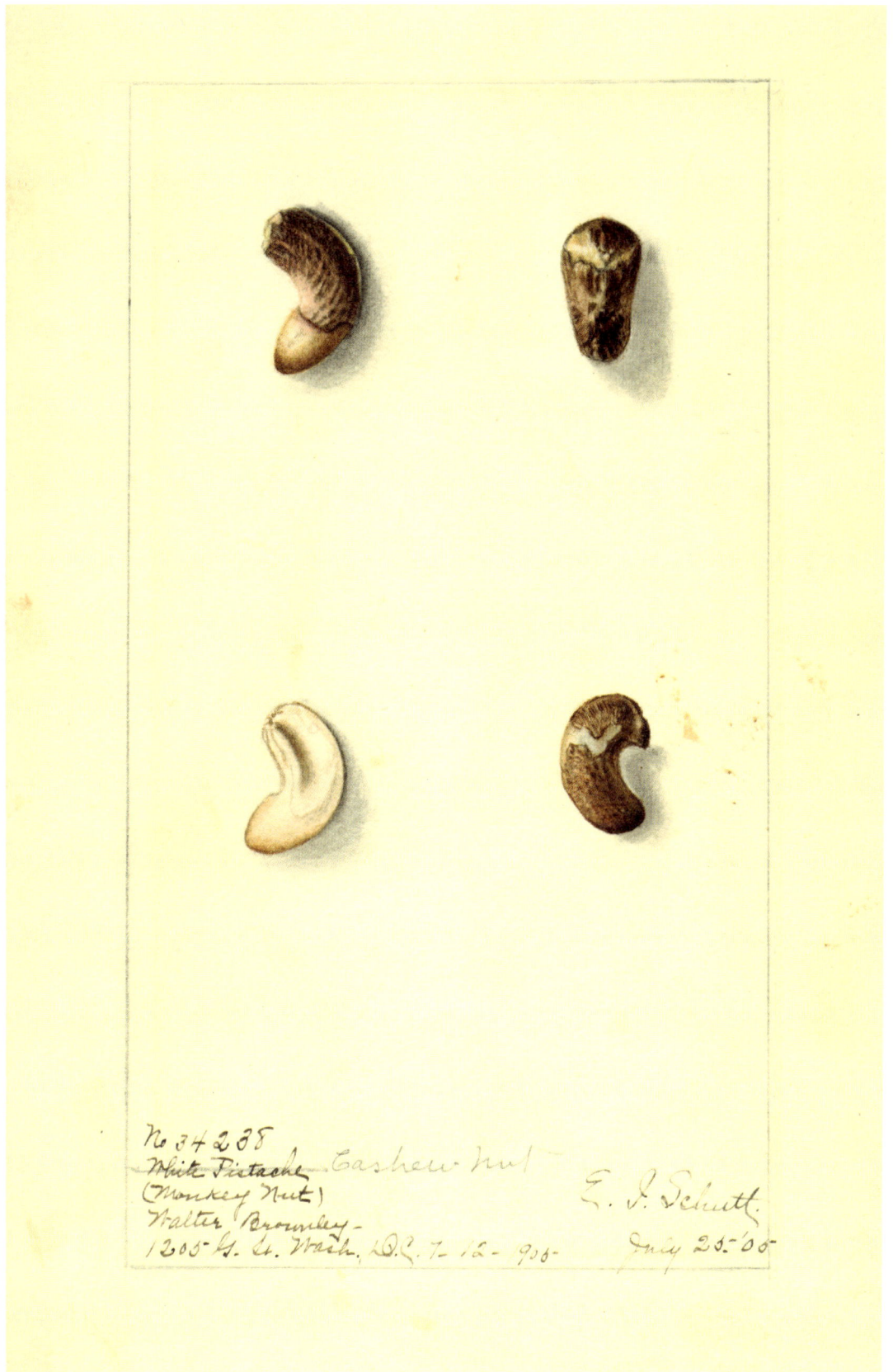

CASHEW NUT
Nº 34238
Anacardium occidentale
Washington, DC, USA
E. I. Schutt, 1905

On the illustration the name Whits Pistache was written and then crossed out. This specimen is also called monkey nut.

56419
Jap Walnut
Arlington Farm,
Rosslyn Va.

J.A. Newton
5-1910

JAPANESE WALNUT

Nº 56419

Juglans ailantifolia

Rosslyn, Arlington County,
Virginia, USA

A. A. Newton, 1910

The Japanese walnut has an oily texture and its husks are
used to produce a yellow tinted dye.

CASHEW NUT
Nº 28932
Anacardium occidentale
Washington, DC, USA
D. G. Passmore, 1903

HAZELNUT
Nº 1344
Corylus
Bell, Prince Georges County,
Maryland, USA
J. M. Shull, 1924

The top leaf is the Prolific hazelnut, given by J. W. Riggs
from Waterloo, Kansas. The bottom leaf is the Gente des
Halles from Chico, collected by E. A. S. from Bell Maryland.

HAZELNUT, KOREAN
Nº 35701
Corylus
Japan
D. G. Passmore, 1906

This specimen was received from David Fairchild at the USDA, Shipping Point Inspection.

No. 94802
Mission
L. G. Dyer
Arndt place
National City, Calif.

R. C. Steadman.
12 – 6 – '17
12 – 1 – '17

OLIVE, MISSION
Nº 94802
Olea europaea
National City, San Diego County,
California, USA
R. C. Steadman, 1917

No. 94909
Manzanillo
C. L. Dyer
Elsinore, Cal.

R. G. Steadman.
12-15-'17
12-13-'17

OLIVE, MANZANILLO
Nº 94909
Olea europaea
Lake Elsinore, Riverside County,
California, USA
R. C. Steadman, 1917

The location was changed from Elsinore to Lake Elsinore in
the archive.

ST JOHN'S BREAD
№ 38302
Ceratonia siliqua L.
Miami, Dade County,
Florida, USA
D. G. Passmore, 1907

St John's bread is an English name for carob, which is also occasionally called the locust tree.

NUTMEG
Nº 36322
Myristica fragrans
Puerto Rico, USA
D. G. Passmore, 1906

This specimen was received from H. G. Henrickson from the Puerto Rico Experiment Station. Nutmeg can also be called *Eugenia malaccensis*, Porto Rico fruit, Malay apple, and *Myristica machate*.

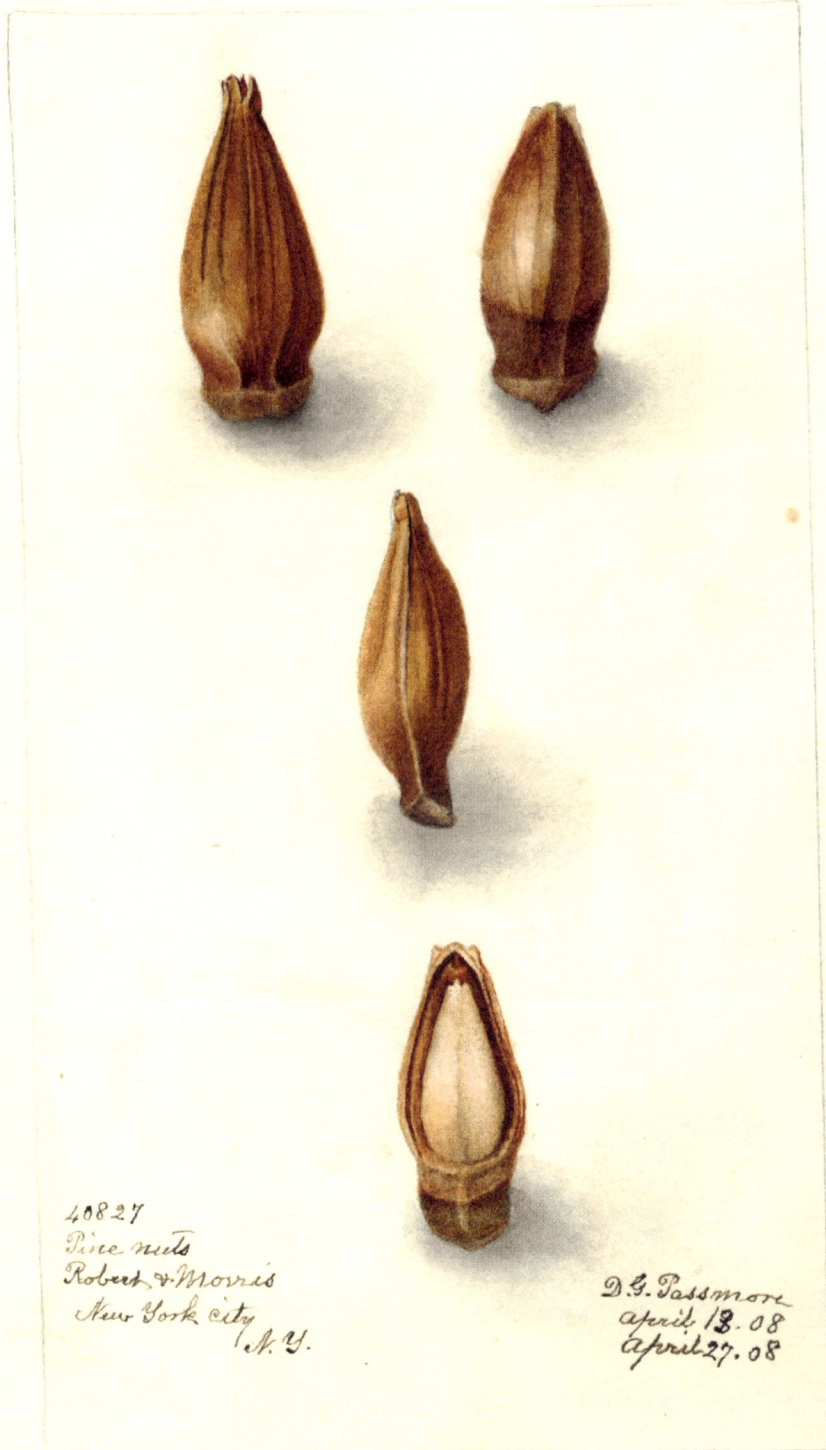

40827
Pine nuts
Robert & Morris
New York city
N. Y.

D. G. Passmore
April 13. 08
April 27. 08

ITALIAN STONE PINE
N° 40827
Pinus pinea
New York, New York, USA
D. G. Passmore, 1908

PEANUT
Nº 40770
Arachis
South Salem, Ross County,
Ohio, USA
A. A. Newton, 1909

The peanut was famously farmed by both former Presidents Thomas Jefferson and Jimmy Carter. Jefferson was the first president to grow the nut, while Carter's family were known peanut farmers who owned a 360-acre farm. Carter himself as a child began selling peanuts on the streets in his neighborhood of Plains in Georgia.

(top) PRICKLY PEAR, Nº 40506, *Opuntia*, San Saba, San Saba County, Texas, USA.
D. G. Passmore, 1908. *(bottom left)* PRICKLY PEAR, Nº 32340, *Opuntia*, Eastlake Park,
Los Angeles, Los Angeles County, California, USA. D. G. Passmore, 1904. *(bottom right)* ROSE
PRICKLY PEAR, Nº 32338, *Opuntia*, Eastlake Park, Los Angeles, Los Angeles County,
California, USA. D. G. Passmore, 1904. This speciment is noted as being Rose Large No. 1.

PRICKLY PEAR
No 17334
Opuntia
Washington, DC, USA
D. G. Passmore, 1899

This specimen was obtained in Bermuda. The prickly pear is described as having a taste that is a combination of bubblegum and watermelon. The sweet fruit can be found growing in abundance in central and western Mexico, where it is also seen adorning the country's coat of arms due to its representation of hope and endurance.

Apples & Oranges

363

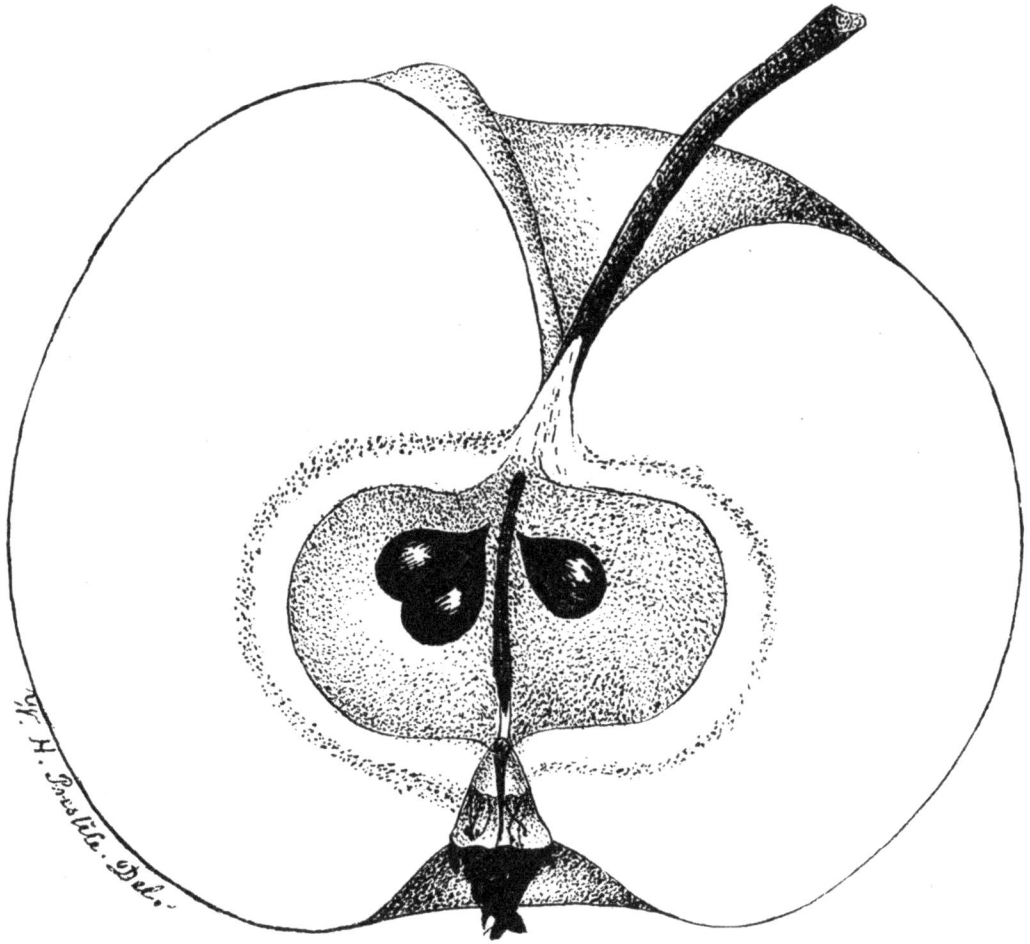

Illustration of a Borovinka
apple, specimen N° 00061, by
W. H. Prestele, 1888.

A pomological path to making sense of the world

Insights from writers writing about fruit

BY Jacqueline Landey

"Citron does not come from true seed. If you plant an orange seed, a grapefruit might spring up."[1] So writes John McPhee in *Oranges,* his fascinating exploration of that apparently ordinary table fruit. "A single citrus tree," he explains, "can be turned into a carnival, with lemons, limes, grapefruits, tangerines, kumquats, and oranges all ripening on its branches at the same time."[2]

The image conjured is of something fantastical, as if from a child's drawing. Such a picture could be hung seamlessly among a wall of kindergarten artworks—so frequently rich in botanical misplacement—where bunches of grapes are crayoned onto oak trees and bright yellow pineapples are scribbled onto palm trees. But the carnival of citrus that McPhee enlightens us with is all the more wonderful in that it is real.

The great Victorian art critic and philosopher John Ruskin lauded the idea of drawing as a means of seeing truly. In his seminal *Elements of Drawing,* he wrote that his chief aim was for the pupil to obtain "a delicate method of work, such as may insure his seeing truly [...] the sight is a more important thing than the drawing; and I would rather teach drawing that my pupils learn to love Nature, than teach the looking at Nature that they may learn to draw."[3] This advice is still acted on today in amateur drawing classes the world over, whenever a lonely apple is placed on a plinth and students are told to draw only what they see. Looking carefully, they shade the gradations of the apple's surface, mark each speckle, recreate the darkness of the hollow at the stem. In this process the students are encouraged to forget what they know or expect in an effort to really see. In another such activity, an art teacher may turn a reference image upside down to help students to sketch it more accurately.

A similar exercise is practiced in writing classes. To inspire clear and original prose, budding writers are asked to describe something familiar, a piece of fruit for instance, to a creature from outer space. Pioneering botanists had a similar writing challenge in describing unfamiliar specimens on expeditions. In Australia in 1770, Joseph Banks wrote in his journal about "something resembling a heart cherry only the stone was soft (*Eugenia*) which had nothing but a light acid to recommend it" and of "a fruit we calld Plumbs, like them in Colour but flat like a little cheese, and another much like a damson both in appearance and taste; both these last however were so full of a large stone that eating them was but an unprofitable business."[4] He wrote of another "so unwholesome" that those that tried it "tho forewarnd [...] were violently affected by them both upwards and downwards."[5]

Where the task of botanists was to make the strange familiar, more contemporary writers writing on fruit, in a world of widely distributed produce, must make the familiar strange. A fresh description brings the fruit right into the room. Oscar Wilde brought us pomegranates which had "split and cracked with the heat, and showed their bleeding hearts."[6] Wallace Stevens gave us peaches, "large and round, Ah! And red; and they have peach fuzz, ah! They are full of juice and the skin is soft. / They are full of the colors of my village / And of fair weather, summer, dew, peace."[7] NoViolet Bulawayo presents bull guavas "big, like a man's fist [...] green on the outside, pink and fluffy on the inside. They taste so good I cannot even explain it."[8] After gorging on these stolen guavas, the characters in this story are "violently affected" as were Joseph Banks' friends.

Like the forbidden fruit of the tree of knowledge in the Garden of Eden, fruit often features as a narrative device in propelling a story forward, or as a catalyst to a character's growth. (In Eric Carle's beloved children's book *The Very Hungry Caterpillar*, literally so.) The sweetness of fruit makes it an appropriate device for showing tensions between childhood and maturity, temptation and resistance, joy and repression. In Peter Carey's *Oscar and Lucinda*, tasting the spiced fruit cake is the pivot on which Oscar turns from his father's religion. The pudding contains cherries, which Oscar has never before seen, raisins, and "a single precious orange." His father calls it "the fruit of Satan" but "Oscar had tasted the pudding. It did not taste like the fruit of Satan."[9]

Through metaphor and symbolism, writers imbue fruit with wide-ranging meanings. For Sylvia Plath, a fig tree could illustrate the paralysis of indecision: "I saw my life branching out before me like the green fig tree..."[10] In Jeannette Winterson's *Oranges are Not the Only Fruit*, the orange symbolizes heteronormativity. In Paul Beatty's *The Sellout*, watermelons are used to satirize the derogatory racist representations that proliferated around the Emancipation Proclamation.[11]

As all fruits exist within social, cultural, and agricultural contexts, each kind of fruit inevitably represents different things in different historical periods. Though freely available in cans today, in 18th-century England, pineapples were very rare, and so, in novels of the period, they signal aristocratic wealth and status, being displays rather than offerings to dinner guests.[12]

Our understanding of fruit is not only laden with social and cultural associations but also personal memories and preferences. And how we see fruit relates to these experiences and our exposure to their many representations.

Reading John McPhee's *Oranges* and Michael Pollen's "The Apple" in his illuminating *The Botany of Desire* offers the opportunity to see the everyday orange and the humble apple in a fresh light. These writings offer insights into the origins of the fruits, their agricultural and social histories, uses around the world, how they are grown, how that process has been industrialized, and how they have become homogenized. These investigations reveal the role marketing has played in public perceptions of the fruits and explore the myths surrounding them. These writers take the apparently familiar and reveal the extraordinary in them. The following excerpts put the orange and the apple on a metaphorical plinth and invite you to take a good look. After reading these pieces, oranges and apples may appear anew—as to a sketcher in Ruskin's drawing class—and how you never thought to see them before.

References

1. McPhee J. (1967) *Oranges*. Farrar, Straus and Giroux, New York. Reprint (2000) Daunt Books, London, p. xv.

2. McPhee J. (1967) *Oranges*. Farrar, Straus and Giroux, New York. Reprint (2000) Daunt Books, London, pp. 21–22.

3. Ruskin J. (1857) *The Elements of Drawing*. Smith, Elder, London, p. xiii. Project Gutenberg, http://www.gutenberg.org/files/30325/30325-h/30325-h.htm.

4. Banks J. (1768–1771) *The Endeavour Journal of Joseph Banks*, vol. 2, Mitchell Library, State Library of New South Wales, Sydney, p. 259. https://setis.library.usyd.edu.au/ozlit/banks/banksvo2.pdf.

5. Banks J. (1768–1771) *The Endeavour Journal of Joseph Banks*, vol. 2, Mitchell Library, State Library of New South Wales, Sydney, p. 286. https://setis.library.usyd.edu.au/ozlit/banks/banksvo2.pdf.

6. Wilde O. (1891) The birthday of the Infanta. In: *A House of Pomegranates*. Methuen, London, p. 31. Project Gutenberg, https://www.gutenberg.org/files/873/873-h/873-h.htm.

7. Stevens W. (1939) A Dish of Peaches in Russia. *Poetry* 54(4), p. 180. https://www.poetryfoundation.org/poetrymagazine/browse?volume=54&issue=4&page=4.

8. Bulawayo N. (2010) Hitting Budapest. *Boston Review* 35(6), pp. 43–47. http://bostonreview.net bulawayo-hitting-budapest.

9. Carey P. (1988) *Oscar and Lucinda*. Harper and Row, New York. Reprint (2010) Faber and Faber, London, p. 10.

10. Plath S. (1963) *The Bell Jar*. Faber and Faber, London, Chapter 7. Project Gutenberg, https://www.gutenberg.ca/ebooks/plaths-belljar/plaths-belljar-00-h.html.

11. Black W. R. (2014) How watermelons became a racist trope. *The Atlantic*, https://www.theatlantic.com/national/archive/2014/12/how-watermelons-became-a-racist-trope/383529.

12. Beauman F. (2006) *The Pineapple: King of Fruits*. Vintage, London.

The Apple

BY Michael Pollan

If you happened to find yourself on the banks of the Ohio River on a particular afternoon in the spring of 1806—somewhere just to the north of Wheeling, West Virginia, say—you would probably have noticed a strange makeshift craft drifting lazily down the river. At the time, this particular stretch of the Ohio, wide and brown and bounded on both sides by steep shoulders of land thick with oaks and hickories, fairly boiled with river traffic, as a ramshackle armada of keelboats and barges ferried settlers from the comparative civilization of Pennsylvania to the wilderness of the Northwest Territory.

The peculiar craft you'd have caught sight of that afternoon consisted of a pair of hollowed-out logs that had been lashed together to form a rough catamaran, a sort of canoe plus sidecar. In one of the dugouts lounged the figure of a skinny man of about thirty, who may or may not have been wearing a burlap coffee sack for a shirt and a tin pot for a hat. According to the man in Jefferson County who deemed the scene worth recording, the fellow in the canoe appeared to be snoozing without a care in the world, evidently trusting in the river to take him wherever it was he wanted to go. The other hull, his sidecar, was riding low in the water under the weight of a small mountain of seeds that had been carefully blanketed with moss and mud to keep them from drying out in the sun.

The fellow snoozing in the canoe was John Chapman, already well known to people in Ohio by his nickname: Johnny Appleseed. He was on his way to Marietta, where the Muskingum River pokes a big hole into the Ohio's northern bank, pointing straight into the heart of the Northwest Territory. Chapman's plan was to plant a tree nursery along one of that river's as-yet-unsettled tributaries, which drain the fertile, thickly forested hills of central Ohio as far north as Mansfield. In all likelihood, Chapman was coming from Allegheny County in western Pennsylvania, to which he returned each year to collect apple seeds, separating them out from the fragrant mounds of pomace that rose by the back door of every cider mill. A single bushel of apple seeds would have been enough to plant more than three hundred thousand trees; there's no way of telling how many bushels of seed Chapman had in tow that day, but it's safe to say his catamaran was bearing several whole orchards into the wilderness.

The image of John Chapman and his heap of apple seeds riding together down the Ohio has stayed with me since I first came across it a few years ago in an out-of-print biography. The scene, for me, has the resonance of myth—a myth about how plants and people learned to use each other, each doing for the other things they could not do for themselves, in the bargain changing each other and improving their common lot.

Henry David Thoreau once wrote that "it is remarkable how closely the history of the apple tree is connected with that of man," and much of the American chapter of that story can be teased out of Chapman's story. It's the story of how pioneers like him helped domesticate the frontier by seeding it with Old World plants. "Exotics," we're apt to call these species today in disparagement, yet without them the American wilderness might never have become a home. What did the apple get in return? A golden age: untold new varieties and half a world of new habitat.

As an emblem of the marriage between people and plants, the design of Chapman's peculiar craft strikes me as just right, implying as it does a relation of parity and reciprocal exchange between its two passengers. More than most of us do, Chapman seems to have had a knack for looking at the world from the plants' point of view—"pomocentrically," you might say. He understood he was working for the apples as much as they were working for him. Perhaps that's why he sometimes likened himself to a bumblebee, and why he would rig up his boat the way he did. Instead of towing his shipment of seeds behind him, Chapman lashed the two hulls together so they would travel down the river side by side.

We give ourselves altogether too much credit in our dealings with other species. Even the power over nature that domestication supposedly represents is overstated. It takes two to perform that particular dance, after all, and plenty of plants and animals have elected to sit it out. Try as they might, people have never been able to domesticate the oak tree, whose highly nutritious acorns remain far too bitter for humans to eat. Evidently the oak has such a satisfactory arrangement with the squirrel—which obligingly forgets where it has buried every fourth acorn or so (admittedly, the estimate is Beatrix Potter's)—that the tree has never needed to enter into any kind of formal arrangement with us.

The apple has been far more eager to do business with humans, and perhaps nowhere more so than in America. Like generations of other immigrants before and after, the apple has made itself at home here. In fact, the apple did such a convincing job of this that most of us wrongly assume the plant is a native. (Even Ralph Waldo Emerson, who knew a thing or two about natural history, called it "the American fruit.") Yet there is a sense—a biological, not just metaphorical sense—in which this is, or has become, true, for the apple transformed itself when it came to America. Bringing boatloads of seed onto the frontier, Johnny Appleseed had a lot to do with that process, but so did the apple itself. No mere passenger or dependent, the apple is the hero of its own story.

This text opens author Michael Pollan's 2002 book *The Botany of Desire* (Random House), which presents case studies that mirror four types of human desires that are reflected in the way that we selectively grow, breed, and genetically engineer our plants.

Oranges

BY John McPhee

The custom of drinking orange juice with breakfast is not very widespread, taking the world as a whole, and it is thought by many peoples to be a distinctly American habit. But many Danes drink it regularly with breakfast, and so do Hondurans, Filipinos, Jamaicans, and the wealthier citizens of Trinidad and Tobago. The day is started with orange juice in the Colombian Andes, and, to some extent, in Kuwait. Bolivians don't touch it at breakfast time, but they drink it steadily for the rest of the day. The "play lunch," or morning tea, that Australian children carry with them to school is usually an orange, peeled spirally halfway down, with the peel replaced around the fruit. The child unwinds the peel and holds the orange as if it were an ice-cream cone. People in Nepal almost never peel oranges, preferring to eat them in cut quarters, the way American athletes do. The sour oranges of Afghanistan customarily appear as seasoning agents on Afghan dinner tables. Squeezed over Afghan food, they cut the grease. The Shamouti Orange, of Israel, is seedless and sweet, has a thick skin, and grows in Hadera, Gaza, Tiberias, Jericho, the Jordan Valley, and Jaffa; it is exported from Jaffa, and for that reason is known universally beyond Israel as the Jaffa Orange. The Jaffa Orange is the variety that British people consider superior to all others, possibly because Richard the Lionhearted spent the winter of 1191-92 in the citrus groves of Jaffa. Citrus trees are spread across the North African coast from Alexandria to Tangier, the city whose name was given to tangerines. Oranges tend to become less tart the closer they are grown to the equator, and in Brazil there is one kind of orange that has virtually no acid in it at all. In the principal towns of Trinidad and Tobago, oranges are sold on street corners. The vender cuts them in half and sprinkles salt on them. In Jamaica, people halve oranges, get down on their hands and knees, and clean floors with one half in each hand. Jamaican mechanics use oranges to clear away grease and oil. The blood orange of Spain, its flesh streaked with red, is prized throughout Europe. Blood oranges grow well in Florida, but they frighten American women. Spain has about thirty-five million orange trees, grows six billion oranges a year, and exports more oranges than any other country, including the United States. In the Campania region of Italy, land is scarce; on a typical small patch, set on a steep slope, orange trees are interspersed with olive and walnut trees, grapes are trained to cover trellises overhead, and as many as five different vegetables are grown on the ground below. The over-all effect is that a greengrocer's shop is springing out of the hillside. Italy produces more than four billion oranges a year, but most of its citrus industry is scattered in gardens of one or two acres. A Frenchman sits at the dinner table, and, as the finishing flourish of

370

the meal, slowly and gently disrobes an orange. In France, peeling the fruit is not yet considered an inconvenience. French preferences run to the blood oranges and the Thomson Navels of Spain, and to the thick-skinned, bland *Maltaises,* which the French import not from Malta but from Tunisia. France itself only grows about four hundred thousand oranges each year, almost wholly in the Department of the *Alpes Maritimes.* Sometimes, Europeans eat oranges with knives and forks. On occasion, they serve a dessert orange that has previously been peeled with such extraordinary care that strips of the peel arc outward like the petals of a flower from the separated and reassembled segments in the center. The Swiss sometimes serve oranges under a smothering of sugar and whipped cream; on a hot day in a Swiss garden, orange juice with ice is a luxurious drink. Norwegian children like to remove the top of an orange, make a little hole, push a lump of sugar into it, and then suck out the juice. English children make orangepeel teeth and wedge them over their gums on Halloween. Irish children take oranges to the movies, where they eat them while they watch the show, tossing the peels at each other and at the people on the screen. In Reykjavik, Iceland, in greenhouses that are heated by volcanic springs, orange trees yearly bear fruit. In the New York Botanical Garden, six mature orange trees are growing in the soil of the Bronx. Their trunks are six inches in diameter, and they bear well every year. The oranges are for viewing and are not supposed to be picked. When people walk past them, however, they sometimes find them irresistible.

The first known reference to oranges occurs in the second book of the *Five Classics,* which appeared in China around 500 B.C. and is generally regarded as having been edited by Confucius. The main course of the migration of the fruit-from its origins near the South China Sea, down into the Malay Archipelago, then on four thousand miles of ocean current to the east coast of Africa, across the desert by caravan and into the Mediterranean basin, then over the Atlantic to the American continents-closely and sometimes exactly kept pace with the major journeys of civilization. There were no oranges in the Western Hemisphere before Columbus himself introduced them. It was Pizarro who took them to Peru. The seeds the Spaniards carried came from trees that had entered Spain as a result of the rise of Islam. The development of orange botany owes something to Vasco da Gama and even more to Alexander the Great; oranges had symbolic importance in the paintings of Renaissance masters; in other times, at least two overwhelming invasions of the Italian peninsula were inspired by the visions of paradise that oranges engendered in northern minds. Oranges were once the fruit of the gods, to whom they were the golden apples of the Hesperides, which were stolen by Hercules. Then, in successive declensions, oranges became the fruit of emperors and kings, of the upper prelacy, of the aristocracy, and, by the eighteenth century, of the rich bourgeoisie. Another hundred years went by before they came within reach of the middle classes, and not until early in this century did they at last become a fruit of the community.

This text opens author John McPhee's 1967 book *Oranges* (Farrar, Straus and Giroux). Originally composed for *The New Yorker,* the reportage explores oranges, their varieties, their history, and how they are grown, particularly in Florida.

Appendix

Glossary

A

Acid rain

Acid rain falls when sulfur dioxide and nitrogen oxide react with water, oxygen, and carbon dioxide in the atmosphere. Acid rain burns plants, affecting growth and causing yellowing of the veins in plants' leaves.

Achene

Any variety of small, dry, hard, one-seeded fruit that doesn't split to release its seeds.

Anthracnose

A small group of fungal diseases which affect a variety of plants in warm, humid areas. It is a disease which causes wilting, withering, and the death of plant tissue. It is characterized especially by necrotic lesions.

B

Berry

In botany, a fleshy fruit without a stone produced from a single flower containing one ovary, such as grapes, currants, tomatoes, cucumbers, eggplants, and bananas, but excluding certain fruits that meet the culinary definition of berries, such as strawberries and raspberries.

Blight

A disease or an injury of a plant which is marked by the formation of lesions, withering, and the death of leaves and tubers. Blight is caused by organisms such as insects or fungus.

Botanical substances

Substances obtained or derived from a plant. Such substances, when extracted, can be used as ingredients in many things, including cosmetic products and medicines, and as flavoring agents.

C

Canker

A destructive fungal disease of apples and other trees that results in an erosive or spreading sore which damages the bark.

Carpel

The female reproductive organ of a flower, consisting of an ovary, a stigma, and usually a style. It may occur singly or as one of a group.

Cherimoya

A round, oblong, or sometimes heart-shaped fruit with a pitted pale green rind. It is the fruit of a tropical American tree (*Annona cherimoya*) of the custard apple family.

Chimera

In botany, it is defined as a plant or plant part that is a mixture of two or more genetically differing types of cells.

Citrus

A tart-to-sweet pulpy fruit with a smooth, shiny, stippled skin. Th fruits grow on any small tree or spiny shrub of the genus *Citrus*, of the Àrue family. They include the lemon, lime, orange, tangerine, grapefruit, citron, kumquat, and shaddock. Often these fruits are widely cultivated as food or grown ornamentally.

Cross-pollinate

A process that involves pollen (the powder produced by the male part of a flower) being carried from one plant to another by the wind or insects.

Cultivars

A variety of a plant that is produced from a natural species and also maintained by ongoing cultivation. A cultivated variety.

Cucurbitaceae family

Part of the larger gourd family, Cucurbitaceaeà are herbaceous climbing vine plants. These plants often have flowers which are unisex and produce large fruits including cucumbers, squash, and melons.

D

Deforestation

The act by humans of cutting down large areas of trees, or the destruction of entire forests.

Drupes

In botany, a drupe is classified as a fleshy fruit with thin skin that usually contains a single seed, including cherries, peaches, and olives. A drupe comes from a single ovary of an individual flower.

E

Ecosystem

A biological community of interacting organisms and their physical environments. It is a complex system of interlocking networks.

Exanthema

A blotch or excrescence on the surface of a leaf.

Exotic plant

A plant that has been introduced to an area outside its natural range.

F

Ferment

Any group of living organisms, such as yeast, molds, and certain bacteria that cause sugars to change into ethyl alcohol due to a reaction involving enzymes.

Fruit grove

A small orchard or stand commonly of citrus-fruit-bearing trees.

G

Gene banks

A collection of seeds, plants, and tissue cultures from potentially useful species. These collections often contain genes which are significant in the breeding of crops.

Germplasm

The genetic material of germ cells. This material can be collected and stored for use in breeding, conservation, and research.

Graft

The act of joining together plant parts through tissue regeneration. This is achieved by joining a portion of one plant (bud or scion) to the stem, root, or branch of another in a way that encourages the continuation of growth. This process is a commonly used vegetation propagation method.

H

Horticulture

The growing of garden crops, typically fruits, vegetables, and ornamental plants.

I

Indehiscent

A fruit which does not open to release seeds.

Indigenous

Native to a particular region and environment.

Interbreed

To crossbreed or mate plants or animals with closely related varieties or specimens.

L

Legume

Also known as a pod, a legume is the fruit of a plant within the pea family. These fruits are characterized by their releasing of seeds as they split along two seams.

Lithograph

A print taken from a planar surface, such as smooth stone or plate metal, onto which the image to be printed is made ink-receptive and the areas to be left blank are made ink-repellent.

N

Nomenclature

A system for naming things in a specific area of science, or the names of things within such a system.

Nursery

A place in which plants are grown for transplanting, for use as stock for budding and grafting, or for sale. Most nursery-grown plants are ornamental, but nurseries also produce and sell fruit plants and other perennial

vegetables to be cultivated further in home gardens.

Nuts

In botany, a nut is a dry, hard fruit that does not split open to release its seed at the point of maturity. A nut resembles an achene but develops from one or more carpels. Examples of true nuts are the chestnut, hazelnut, and acorn.

O

Orange rust

A disease of raspberries and blackberries caused by two types of rust fungus, *Gymnoconia peckiana* and *Kunkelia nitens*, commonly characterized by orange powder on the undersides of leaves and stunted or misshapen foliage.

Orchard

An area of land in which fruit trees, excluding orange or other citrus trees, are grown— an apple or cherry orchard, for instance.

P

Pistil

The female reproductive part of a flower typically consisting of the ovary, which contains the potential seeds (or ovules), a stalk (or style) arising from the ovary, and the stigma (pollen-receptive tip).

Pomes

The characteristic fruit of the apple family, including apples, pears, and quinces.

Pomology

A branch of horticulture which is focused on the study and cultivation of fruit.

Pruning

In horticulture, pruning is defined as the removal or reduction of parts of a plant, tree, or vine that are seen as

injurious or no longer required for the growth, production, or development of that plant. Pruning can also help to enhance the shape of a plant while encouraging new growth.

S

Scab

In botany, scab is defined as a bacterial or fungal plant disease that can be characterized by crustaceous lesions on the fruit, tubers, leaves, or stems.

Scion

The detached, living part of a plant, such as a bud, which is cut for grafting or rooting.

Seed vault

A place used for the storage of seeds as a source for planting against the event of seed reserves or biodiversity failing elsewhere.

Seedling

A young plant grown from seed. The word is also used to describe a young tree before it becomes a sapling or a nursery plant waiting to be transplanted.

Specimen

An individual plant that is used to show or be examined as an example of its variety for scientific study.

Stone fruit

The non-technical name for a drupe that refers to any fruit that has a stone, such as a plum.

Subtropical fruit

Subtropical fruits are native to the areas adjacent to or bordering on the Tropics of Cancer and Capricorn. These include citrus fruits, dates, olives, pomegranates, grapes, figs, and persimmons.

T

Taxonomy

The scientific study of naming, defining, and classifying groups of biological organisms based on shared characteristics.

Tropical fruit

Fruits native to the Tropics of Cancer and Capricorn such as guava, mango, papaya, and pineapple.

U

Urban sprawl

Rapid expansion of cities and towns, often characterized by low-density residential housing.

V

Vine

Any plant that has a long, slender stem that either trails on the ground or climbs by winding around a support to which it attaches itself with tendrils.

Index

Further Reading

American Pomological Society and US Bureau of Plant Industry (1909) *Fruits Recommended by the American Pomological Society for Cultivation in the Various Sections of the United States and Canada. Rev. by a Committee of the American Pomological Society, W. H. Ragan, Chairman.* US GPO, Washington, DC.

Beauman F. (2006) *The Pineapple: King of Fruits.* Vintage, London.

Bunyard E. A. (1929) *The Anatomy of Dessert.* Dulau, London

Bussey D. J. and Whealy K. (eds) (2016) *The Illustrated History of Apples in the United States and Canada,* 7 volumes. JAK KAW Press, Mount Horeb, WI.

Calhoun C. L. (2011) *Old Southern Apples: A Comprehensive History and Description of Varieties for Collectors, Growers, and Fruit Enthusiasts,* revised and expanded edition. Chelsea Green, White River Junction, VT.

Cronenwett P. N. (2007) *Celebrating Research: Rare and Special Collections from the Membership of the Association of Research Libraries.* Association of Research Libraries, Washington, DC.

Cronquist A. (1968) *The Evolution and Classification of Flowering Plants.* Houghton Mifflin, Boston, MA.

Cunningham I. S. (1984) *Frank N. Meyer: Plant Hunter in Asia.* Iowa State University Press, Ames, IA.

Davidson A. (1991) *Fruit: A Connoisseur's Guide and Cookbook.* Mitchell Beazley, London.

Davidson A. (1999) *The Oxford Companion to Food.* Oxford University Press, Oxford.

de Candolle A. P. (1884) *Origin of Cultivated Plants.* Kegan Paul, Trench, Trübner, London.

Downing A. J. (1882) *The Fruits and Fruit-trees of America, or, The Culture, Propagation and Management, in the Garden and Orchard, of Fruit-trees Generally: With Descriptions of All the Finest Varieties of Fruit, Native and Foreign, Cultivated in this Country.* John Wiley & Sons, New York, NY.

Fairchild D. G. (1930) *Exploring for Plants.* Macmillan, New York, NY.

Fairchild D. G. Kay A., and Kay E. (1939) *The World Was My Garden: Travels of a Plant Explorer.* Scribner, New York, NY.

Ferree D. C. and Chandler L. E. (1998) *A History of Fruit Varieties: The American Pomological Society: One Hundred and Fifty Years, 1848–1998.* Good Fruit Grower Magazine, Yakima, WA.

Fusonie A. E. (1990) The heritage of original art and photo imaging in USDA: past, present and future. *Agricultural History* 64(2), pp. 300–314.

Hedrick U. P., New York State Agricultural Experiment Station, and New York (State) Department of Agriculture (1911) *The Plums of New York.* J. B. Lyon, Albany, NY.

Hedrick U. P., Howe G. H., and New York State Agricultural Experiment Station (1925) *The Small Fruits of New York.* J. B. Lyon, Albany, NY.

Hogg R. (1859) *The Apple and its Varieties: Being a History and Description of the Varieties of Apples Cultivated in the Gardens and Orchards of Great Britain.* Groombridge & Sons, London.

Kirker M. and Newman C. L. (2020) Cherry. Reaktion Books, London.

McPhee J. (1967) *Oranges.* Farrar, Straus and Giroux, New York. Reprint (2000) Daunt Books, London.

New York (State) Department of Agriculture *et al.* (1905) *The Apples of New York,* vols I and II. J. B. Lyon, Albany, NY.

New York (State) Department of Agriculture *et al.* (1908) *The Grapes of New York.* J. B. Lyon, Albany, NY.

New York (State) Department of Agriculture *et al.* (1915) *The Cherries of New York.* J. B. Lyon, Albany, NY.

New York State Agricultural Experiment Station *et al.* (1917) *The Peaches of New York.* J. B. Lyon, Albany, NY.

New York State Agricultural Experiment Station *et al.* (1921) *The Pears of New York.* J. B. Lyon, Albany, NY.

Pollan M. (2002) *The Botany of Desire.* Random House, New York, NY.

Ragan W. H. (1904) *Varieties of Fruits Recommended for Planting.* USDA, Washington, DC.

Ragan W. H. (1926) *Nomenclature of the Apple; A Catalogue of the Known Varieties Referred to in American Publications from 1804 to 1904.* US GPO, Washington, DC.

Roberts J. (2001) *The Origins of Fruits and Vegetables.* Universe, New York, NY.

Ruskin J. (1857) *The Elements of Drawing.* Smith, Elder, London.

Schenck A. A. (n.d.) *Condensed Apple Book for Use in the Orchard.* Books 2 and 3 found in USDA Fruit Laboratory Card Files (MS 365), Series IB.

Online Resources

Henry G. Gilbert Nursery and Seed Trade Catalog Collection, 1724–2020. Special Collections, USDA National Agricultural Library. https://archive.org/details/usda-nurseryandseedcatalog

Meyer F. N. (1910) Foreign seed and plant introduction: Crimea, Caucasus, Russian Turkestan: Jan 22, 1910 to July 10, 1910 [photograph album]. Special Collections, USDA National Agricultural Library. https://archive.org/details/CAT31327470

Meyer F. N. (1918) South China explorations: typescript, July 25, 1916–September 21, 1918. Special Collections, USDA National Agricultural Library. https://archive.org/details/CAT10662165MeyerSouthChinaExplorations

Secretary of Agriculture (1886–1942) *Report of the Secretary of Agriculture*. Government Printing Office, Washington, DC. https://archive.org/details/usda-reportofsecretaryofagriculture

USDA (1918) *Program of Work of the United States Department of Agriculture for the Fiscal Year 1919*. USDA, Washington, DC, pp. 214–231. https://archive.org/details/CAT31326086004/page/214/mode/2up

USDA (1967) *Agriculture and the Yearbook of Agriculture, 1849-1967*. USDA, Washington, DC. https://archive.org/details/CAT31335956/page/n1mode/2up?q=annual+report+secretary+of+agriculture+1926

USDA Fruit Laboratory Card Files (MS 365). Special Collections, USDA National Agricultural Library. https://specialcollections.nal.usda.gov/usda-fruit-laboratory-cardfiles

USDA Pomological Watercolor Collection, 1886–1942 (MS 184). Special Collections, USDA National Agricultural Library. https://usdawatercolors.nal.usda.gov/pom/home.xhtml

White J. J. and Neumann E. A. (1982) The collection of pomological watercolors at the U.S. National Arboretum. *Huntia* 4, pp. 103–123. http://www.huntbotanical.org/admin/uploads/03hibd-huntia-4-2-pp103-124.pdf

Related Collections (Artists' Collections) in Special Collections, National Agricultural Library

Deborah Griscom Passmore Watercolors (MS 124). https://specialcollections.nal.usda.gov/guide-collections/ deborah-griscom-passmore-watercolors. Watercolour album (1911): https://archive.org/details/CAT11048856

Royal C. Steadman Watercolor Collection, 1923–1928 (MS 258). https://www.nal.usda.gov/speccoll/collectionsguide/collection2.php?search=Steadman

US National Fungus Collections Topical Files, 1850–1970 (MS 454). (Includes work of artist Louis C. C. Krieger.) https://specialcollections.nal.usda.gov/guide-collections/us-national-fungus-collections-topical-files

Wilhelm Heinrich (William Henry) Prestele Papers, 1887–1891 (MS 137). https://specialcollections.nal.usda.gov/guide-collections/wilhelm-heinrich-william-henry-prestele-papers

Related Collections at the National Archives and Records Administration (NARA), College Park, Maryland

Department of Agriculture (1886–1907) Journals of Receipt and Distribution of New Fruit Specimens, 1886–1907. Record Group 54: Records of the Bureau of Plant Industry, Soils, and Agricultural Engineering, 1853–1977. https://catalog.archives.gov/id/2110752

Department of Agriculture (1886–1941) "Variety Index" to the Series "Journals of Receipt of Fruit Specimens, 1886-1941." Record Group 54: Records of the Bureau of Plant Industry, Soils, and Agricultural Engineering, 1853–1977. https://catalog.archives.gov/id/2110736

Permissions

About the collection

The US Department of Agriculture (USDA) Pomological Watercolor Collection contains 7,584 watercolor paintings of cultivated fruit and nut varieties, alongside specimens gathered around the world and introduced by USDA plant explorers from the late 19th and early 20th centuries. These remarkable, botanically accurate watercolors were painted by 21 professional artists (including ten women) employed by the USDA between 1886 and 1942. Produced largely before the widespread use of photography, the watercolors were created and published to aid identification and examination of fruit varieties, for the nation's fruit growers.

The watercolor collection is preserved in the Special Collections of the National Agricultural Library (NAL), one of five national libraries of the United States. As part of the USDA and the Agricultural Research Service (ARS), the library houses one of the world's largest collections on agriculture and its related sciences. NAL's Special Collections unit preserves and provides access to materials significant to the history of agriculture and the USDA, including rare books and manuscripts, document collections, nursery and seed trade catalogs, photographs, and posters.

Search the complete watercolor collection: usdawatercolors.nal.usda.gov.

Contributors

Adam Leith Gollner

is the author of *The Fruit Hunters* (2008), *The Book of Immortality* (2013), and *Working in the Bathtub* (2020). He has written for *The New York Times*, *The Paris Review*, *Vanity Fair*, *The Smithsonian*, and *The New Yorker* online. He lives in Montreal, Canada.

Jacqueline Landey

is a writer based in London. She completed an MA in creative writing at the University of East Anglia and has been published by Al Jazeera, *National Geographic Traveller* (South Africa), *Shooter Literary Magazine*, Totally Dublin, *ArtThrob*, and Review 31.

John McPhee

is a staff writer at *The New Yorker*, and has taught writing at Princeton University since 1975. He is the author of 33 books, all published by Farrar, Straus and Giroux. His two most recent titles are *Draft No. 4* published in 2017 and *The Patch* published in 2018. He lives in Princeton, New Jersey.

Michael Pollan

is the author of *How to Change Your Mind* (Penguin, 2019), *Cooked* (Penguin, 2014), *Food Rules* (Penguin, 2009), *In Defense of Food* (Penguin, 2009), *The Omnivore's Dilemma* (Penguin, 2007), *The Botany of Desire* (Random House, 2002), *Second Nature* (Grove Press, 2003), and *A Place of My Own* (Penguin, 2008). A longtime contributor to the *New York Times Magazine*, he also teaches writing at Harvard University as well as at the University of California, Berkeley.

Marina Vitaglione

is a photographer, photo editor, and writer based between France and London, UK. She is the author of *Solastalgia* (Overlapse, 2017), a photo/text docufiction on the impact of climate change on Venice, Italy.

Colophon

U

**UNION
SQUARE
& CO.**

NEW YORK

UNION SQUARE & CO. and the distinctive Union Square &
Co. logo are trademarks of Hachette Book Group, Inc.

First published by Atelier Éditions 2021

All Artworks by the artists of the USDA Department
of Pomology
Introduction © 2021 Adam Leith Gollner
Chapter Introductions by Marina Vitaglione
Literary Fruits essay by Jacqueline Landey
Featured Excerpts by John McPhee, Michael Pollan

ISBN 978-1-4549-6353-0

Union Square & Co. books may be purchased in bulk for
business, educational, or promotional use. For more
information, please contact your local bookseller or the
Hachette Book Group's Special Markets department at
special.markets@hbgusa.com.

Printed in Spain

2 4 6 8 10 9 7 5 3 1

unionsquareandco.com

A book by Atelier Éditions
atelier éditions
atelier-editions.com

Editor: Pascale Georgiev
Designer: Capucine Labarthe
Sub-Editor: Gregor Shepherd
Design & Editorial Assistant: Emma Singleton
Art Director: Renée Bollier
Project Editor: Caitlin Leffel
Copyeditor: Rich Cutler, Helius

Acknowledgments
Atelier Éditions wish to extend their immense
gratitude to the National Agricultural Library of the US
Department of Agriculture, especially
to Susan Fugate and the Special Collections Department, who
helped lead our project to fruition.

In exploring the collection, the publisher also wishes to
emphasize the contribution of the USDA's Department of
Pomology's 10 women artists to the science of pomology.
Such enduring contributions to the science of fruit and cultivation remain as significant today as they were throughout the
field's 19th- and 20th-century infancy.